# The
# NATURE
# of
# REST

T0356517

abundant life. Thank you, Eryn, for giving us the liberty to reestablish rest as an important part of our day."

—Jessie Seneca, author, speaker, and founder of
More of Him Ministries

"As a child, many of the moments I felt closest to God happened through nature. As hurried, weary grown-ups, we can still look to creation for reminders of who God is, who we are, and how much we're loved. *The Nature of Rest* is a welcome invitation to draw close to the One who created us and who still cares for us."

—Holley Gerth, *Wall Street Journal* best-selling author of
*365 Truths for Every Woman's Heart*

"In *The Nature of Rest*, Eryn gives us practical tools for reordering and reenergizing our lives. This book does more than just inspire. It goes beyond simply adding rest as another item on our to-do lists and does not hand out unattainable goals that work only for a select few. Instead, Eryn walks us through how to realistically align our lives with God's gift of rest and, in doing so, accomplish more effectively the goals and visions He has given us. I am fully confident that anyone seeking to find God and His rest will find both in the pages of this book."

—Emily Assell, best-selling author of the Generation Claimed series

"For many of us, rest seems elusive. The demands and expectations on our lives seem endless, and yet God calls us to rest. He commands us to rest (Exodus 16:26). So how do we find it? In *The Nature of Rest*, Eryn Lynum invites us to look carefully into God's Word and what He has to say about rest. Not only does Eryn share biblical principles of why we can and should rest, she gently walks us through establishing rhythms and disciplines that can lead us to a life of vitality and deeper trust in God."

—Durenda Wilson, host of *The Durenda Wilson Podcast* and
author of *The Unhurried Homeschooler*

"*The Nature of Rest* gives insight into our need to be intentionally unproductive. In a world that values accomplishment above all else, Eryn Lynum sheds light on our call from God to rest, reflect, and relate. If you are weary from trying to keep up or catch up, you will find that the antidote for a frantic life is found in a discipline of rest."

—Jill Smith, author of *Nature Unveiled: 40 Reflections on Experiencing God's Creation*

"In *The Nature of Rest*, author Eryn Lynum does a masterful job of combining her love for God's written Word with her love for God's created world in a way that invites us all to renounce our life-threatening addiction to busyness and enter more fully into our Lord's 'unforced rhythms of grace.' Drink deeply, my friends. You won't be disappointed."

—David O. Williams, DMin, author of *Rhythms of Grace: Life-Saving Disciplines for Spiritual Leaders*

"Are you like me, where you sometimes (maybe often) feel depleted, hurried, distracted, or restless? If you long for peace and contentment, you need Eryn Lynum's *The Nature of Rest*. Eryn beckons her reader to harmonize rest and activity to be fully alive. She carefully unpacks the spiritual discipline of rest as seen in Scripture and compares it to the natural rhythms of creation. You will discover how to embrace and apply each principle of rest presented. While reading, I felt the blessing of peace settle over me. This book will bless you too."

—Lori Wildenberg, speaker, parent coach, and author of *The Messy Life of Parenting*

"As I understand it, Sabbath keeping isn't a condition of getting into heaven; it's just the condition heaven is in. In *The Nature of Rest*, Eryn Lynum clearly articulates the biblical case for two of the Lord's greatest gifts—the wonders of creation and His invitation to Sabbath rest. *The Nature of Rest* is a life-changing read for anyone seeking abiding peace in today's chaotic world."

—Matthew Sleeth, MD, executive director of
Blessed Earth and author of 24/6

"In our busy lives, where stress and overwhelm are all too common, Lynum's book is a beacon of hope. It's enlightening to realize that our struggle with rest is often rooted in unbelief. This book underscores the importance of rest and provides practical, actionable guidance on how to rest effectively. Lynum's wealth of insightful ideas, woven with biblical wisdom and the divine design of creation, make this a must-read for every family!"

—Lee Ann Mancini, author of *Raising Kids to Follow Christ*,
founder of Raising Christian Kids, adjunct professor at South
Florida Bible College & Theological Seminary, and
executive producer of Sea Kids

"Eryn Lynum is uniquely positioned to write on the power of rest. Diagnosed with a rare condition as a teenager, Eryn literally had to learn how to rest to stay alive. Eryn has studied what the Scriptures and the natural world teach about rest. Her compelling and beautiful book will help you shift from hurry and worry to rest and quiet."

—Arlene Pellicane, author of *Parents Rising* and host of
*The Happy Home Podcast*

"I found *The Nature of Rest* a refreshing study and sensed calmness from the opening pages. Through this study, Eryn shows the biblical meaning of rest and helps us discover rest as a necessity without feeling guilty. Rest is not a bad word but an essential action. I appreciate how she relates God's creation to our everyday existence and shows us how rest not only brings life to our dry bones, but brings

# The
# NATURE
## of
# REST

**WHAT THE BIBLE AND CREATION
TEACH US ABOUT SABBATH LIVING**

ERYN LYNUM

KREGEL
PUBLICATIONS

*The Nature of Rest: What the Bible and Creation Teach Us About Sabbath Living*
© 2025 by Eryn Lynum

Published by Kregel Publications, a division of Kregel Inc., 2450 Oak Industrial Dr. NE, Grand Rapids, MI 49505. www.kregel.com.

Eryn Lynum is represented by and *The Nature of Rest* is published in association with The Steve Laube Agency, LLC. www.stevelaube.com.

The persons and events portrayed in this book have been used with permission.

All Hebrew and Greek translations were taken from either *Strong's Concordance* at Blue Letter Bible (https://www.blueletterbible.org/resources/lexical/strongs-definitions.cfm) or Logos Bible Software (https://support.logos.com/hc/en-us).

Cataloging-in-Publication Data is available from the Library of Congress.

ISBN 978-0-8254-4889-8, print
ISBN 978-0-8254-6370-9, epub
ISBN 978-0-8254-6369-3, Kindle

Printed in the United States of America
25 26 27 28 29 30 31 32 33 34 / 5 4 3 2 1

*For Grayson*
*You always bring me back to restful living and inspire*
*and equip me to live fully alive. Thank you for taking*
*me to quiet, wilderness places often. Thanks for always*
*knowing where to find moose, mountain goats, horned*
*larks, and wild orchids.*


*For Zeke, Ellis, Will, and Roary*
*Thank you for every Sabbath spent reading, playing chess,*
*swimming, enjoying coffee cake, and hiking together. You*
*are my favorite people to rest with.*

# CONTENTS

# WHAT IS VITAL?

HAVE YOU EVER WATCHED A hummingbird busily visiting flowers? Perhaps *visiting* is not the right word, for the bird's effort is hardly leisurely. It is hard work. Recently I watched a black-chinned hummingbird hover around my backyard bird feeders. Above the buzz of his wings, I could nearly hear his grumbling. We were heading into fall, and I'd taken down our hanging flower baskets. After inspecting the opening of the seed feeders and finding no nectar— the sweet liquid from flowers he subsists on—he continued on his way.

The buzzing of his wings reflects a profound design. Hummingbirds beat their wings up to 70 times per second—around 4,200 beats per minute. A hummingbird's heart beats approximately 1,200 times every minute to fuel that constant activity. That's 1,400 percent more than an average human heart rate. Watching a hummingbird whip through the sky, I can relate to his ongoing activity. My pace can feel nonstop. Do you feel this same tension of too much work and constant hustle?

It is easy to move rapidly from one activity to the next throughout our days. But this tiny avian creature also teaches us an essential lesson about rest. To fuel their endeavors, hummingbirds conserve energy through a strategy called *torpor*. The hummingbird becomes unresponsive, and an observer might fear it is dead when, in fact, torpor is what keeps it alive. A lot is happening in the tiny bird that cannot be seen. Their body temperature drops (up to fifty degrees lower than usual), and they enter a deep sleepy state. They dial in this strategy of rest to sustain their pace of life.

What if we, too, could support our lives through regular stops? As God designed the hummingbird with restful rhythms, so has he engineered our lives to operate within patterns of rest and activity, cooperating in vital harmony.

Maybe you feel the deficit of rest. You're not sure what the restful life Jesus speaks about in Matthew 11:28–30 looks like, or how to get there, or if it's realistic. Maybe we have been thinking about rest wrong, as if it's something we must earn through our efforts and work. Or perhaps rest feels lazy, like we're not pulling our weight or staying as productive as those around us.

Reflecting on Jesus's invitation in Matthew 11:28—"Come to me, all who labor and are heavy laden, and I will give you rest"—the late theologian Oswald Chambers wrote this:

> Rest means the *perfection of motion*. "I will give you rest," that is, "I will stay you." Not—"I will put you to bed and hold your hand and sing you to sleep"; but—"I will get you out of bed, out of the languor and exhaustion, out of being half dead while you are alive; I will so imbue you with the spirit of life that you will be stayed by the *perfection of vital activity*."[1]

Stop. Read the quote above again.

This is a unique perspective on rest. Not idle, but active. Not lazy, but effective and impactful.

Have you ever equated rest with being fully alive?

Notice three things:

1. Chambers wrote that God will "stay you." What does it look like to be *stayed*? When God stays us, he is calling us out of

hurry and toward peaceful rest as an anchor for our lives. He assures us it is okay and even necessary to be still, just as we saw with the hummingbird. We can practice letting God stay us as we position ourselves in his love, care, and provision.

2. Chambers asked, Are we living half dead while alive? A restless life can be the effect of extreme FOMO (fear of missing out). We can toil away our days in constant pursuit of *more*. But more what? Jesus's idea of *more* is far greater than anything we can accumulate on earth. As we'll see in the coming weeks, biblical rest is essential to *fully live*. In John 10:10 Jesus called it the "abundant life."

3. Finally, Chambers said rest is the "perfection of vital activity." Rest helps align our daily activities with our deepest values. What is important for you and your family? Do you hold relationships, faith, community, health, or work in high regard? What do you consider essential to your physical, spiritual, and mental wellness? In order to rest, we need to prayerfully reorganize our lives and activities to support what we consider vital.

## Rest in Scripture and Creation

Throughout this study, we will explore examples from nature, like the hummingbird. As a master naturalist, I often come to understand God more deeply through these examples. Growing up in the church and attending Bible college, I learned how to look for God in the Scriptures and dig deeper into the context and original language to glean more from his living and active Word. Years later I became caught up in the wonder of nature and trained as a certified master naturalist to better understand the things God had made. These two areas of study—theology and nature—overlap and synthesize.

God reveals himself to us in two main ways—through Scripture *(special revelation)* and creation *(natural revelation)*. Romans 1:20 attests to the latter: "His invisible attributes, namely, his eternal power and divine nature, have been clearly perceived, ever since the creation of the world, in the things that have been made. . . ."

Although natural revelation is limited and cannot ultimately share the gospel with us, it does have much to teach us about God. It highlights and complements the truths we find in Scripture. We will discover that God has designed rhythms of rest right into the natural world. In creation, we find that rest is essential to life.

In this study we'll dive into Scripture and creation to see what God says about rest, and discover beautiful overlapping layers.

## What Is the Right Kind of Busy?

I wrote this book during my family's busiest year and while also completing other writing assignments, marketing my previous book, managing a rapidly growing podcast, raising and homeschooling four young children, leading community nature programs, and attempting to be a decent wife and mother amid all these responsibilities. Yet regular rhythms of rest steadied me and kept me from frantic or reactive living. Every Friday afternoon I answered lingering emails, then closed my laptop and tucked it away in a closet until Sunday evening. I silenced my phone and put it in a drawer. Sabbath sustained me as torpor sustains the hummingbird. Further, daily rhythms of rest equipped me to faithfully carry out the work God called me to without overextending myself. Beginning my day in his Word rather than my email inbox, enjoying walks around my neighborhood between tasks, and pausing to pray and invite his restful presence into my day reminded me he is the one carrying out this work at his pace, by his power, and for his glory. I can rest and work in vital harmony.

Your list of responsibilities might look different. This season might seem lighter or heavier—that's beside the point, because all of us are busy. Even if our agenda doesn't seem busy, our minds and hearts are. Maybe you're building a career, raising a family, caring for aging parents, serving in ministry or your community, single parenting, attending classes, or a million other things because, in this world, the possibilities for busyness are endless. God designed life to be busy, but are we living the right kind of busy? And more importantly, are rhythms of rest sustaining us in the busyness and complementing the work God calls us to?

## Checking Our Vital Activity

Oswald Chambers called rest the "perfection of vital activity." So the first question we must ask is, What is vital activity?

When you visit a doctor, one of the first things the nurse does is check your vitals—your temperature, blood pressure, pulse, and respiration. These vitals are a telltale if something is wrong.

In my story, the doctor's office and these vital signs were the prelude to a lifelong pursuit of restful living. I was fourteen years old when, during a routine doctor visit, my blood pressure registered critically low, at fifty-eight over forty-six. My vitals were off, and something was undoubtedly wrong. I was soon diagnosed with a rare and potentially fatal condition called Addison's disease, or adrenal insufficiency. My adrenal glands do not function. These glands not only produce their namesake, adrenaline, but also the essential hormone cortisol, which manages stress response—our fight-or-flight response. Exposed to stress, my body does not fight or flee; it fails.

From that early age, I had to learn to live in a stress-filled world while maintaining a calm mind and perspective because stress can literally kill me. In my case, rest is essential to living. This part of my story uniquely qualified me to write this book, because rest is what has helped me fully live. My prayer is it will do the same for you. God designed rest to be vital. And to experience rest, we must decide what in our lives are vital activities, which we will identify in the coming weeks. As we distinguish vital activities, we'll develop a clear picture of what Jesus calls the *abundant* life.

The Enemy uses hurry, hustle, and the fear of missing out to distract us from God's desire for us: extraordinary lives full of purpose and fueled by rest. Jesus made it clear that he wants more for us than an ordinary life spent rushing from one activity to the next as our souls are depleted. He said in John 10:10, "The thief comes only to steal and kill and destroy. I came that they may have life and have it abundantly."

How does the Enemy steal, kill, and destroy? Through hurry and distraction.

How might Jesus offer us abundant life? Through rest.

The word *abundantly* in its original Greek is *perissos* and means "more," "beyond measure," "over and above," "surpassing," "uncommon," and "extraordinary." Chambers said it this way: God would take us "out of being half dead while you are alive" and "so imbue you with the spirit of life."

Amid my busiest season of life, I found rest not because I had nothing to do but because I worked toward the perfection of vital activity. This is a process of refinement and reconciling our activities and rhythms with our values. We need to regularly ask ourselves, What does it look like to perfect vital activity? How can we rest and work in harmony?

The six weeks of this study are designed to help you answer those questions. In weeks 1–3, we will capture God's vision of rest, which is far different from this world's definitions. Then in weeks 4–6, we will turn our lives toward God's rest through biblical practices. God's rest won't be a fanciful idea you hope to experience once the work is done. It won't be an afterthought. Instead, it will become a foundation and lifeblood of your experience. It will help you live fully alive.

## Getting the Most out of This Study

On each day, we'll walk through Scripture and nature. Looking at rest through these two God-given lenses will help us understand and embrace his invitation. After each reading, we'll dive deeper with the following sections:

**The Roots:** Gain a more comprehensive view of Scripture by digging into the original language. This section explores a verse (or two) related to the day's lesson, including its keywords, Hebrew or Greek origins, and pronunciation—you know, in case you want to polish your phonetics. Each keyword includes a few other possible translations and ways the word is used throughout Scripture. This section will help you discover how the roots of rest intertwine all throughout God's Word.

*Example:*
Come with me by yourselves to a quiet place and get some rest. (Mark 6:31 NIV)

Quiet | ἔρημος | *erēmos* | er'-ay-mos | solitary, desolate, wilderness

- *Quiet* is how the word is translated in our selected translation (in this example, NIV).
- ἔρημος is the original Greek.
- *Erēmos* is the transliteration (the in-between step when a word is converted from one writing system to another, to preserve pronunciation).
- Er'-ay-mos is the pronunciation.
- *Solitary*, *desolate*, and *wilderness* are other words this

Greek word is sometimes translated as throughout Scripture, and lend more context to its meaning.

**Rest & Reflect:** Here, record thoughts and prayers as you progress through the day's lesson.

**Under the Microscope:** Practice connecting biblical themes as you mark up a passage and discover keywords, related ideas, and how they all contribute to and strengthen the theme of rest. On some days, this section will offer a conclusive thought on biblical rest, while on other days, it will guide you through an interactive study of a particular passage.

Keep in mind, this study builds on itself. Later lessons will refer to concepts explored in earlier lessons. This is a journey toward a more restful life and fuller experience of God.

Okay. Let's begin.

# WEEK 1

# RESTORE
## A Pattern of Rest

*Thus said the Lord GOD, the Holy One of Israel,*
*"In returning and rest you shall be saved;*
*in quietness and in trust shall be your strength."*

ISAIAH 30:15

# WEEK 1

## *Day 1*

# GOD CREATED REST
# AS A PATTERN

I AM IN AWE EVERY spring as I watch nature wake up and burst into life. Seemingly without effort, bare tree branches fill with leaves, buds, and blossoms. Yet I know this process requires important work and rest.

Unlike annual plants, which audaciously shoot up for a single season, then take a bow and fade into time, perennials bloom year after year. I witness this in my gardens when echinacea, bee balm, columbine, and yarrow send up new sprouts after long winter months. What gives the perennial such a legacy? Like a hummingbird, a perennial's longevity relies on patterns of rest and work. Throughout winter, when it seems as though the whole land is napping, a perennial's roots are gaining strength. During significant seasonal pauses, these plants draw their energy back from the performance of blooming and growing to redirect focus to their roots. Without the vital activity of rest, the plant would be unable to do its work of producing life and beauty year after year.

Rest is integral to God's design of humans as well, which is why it's an essential element of the creation narrative in Genesis 1. You'll note that rest is not a symptom or result of a sin-struck world but a part of God's original blueprint. Before the Serpent slunk in with his lies, God established a pattern of rest. Consider the following time-line of events:

- **Day 1:** God prepared the expanse, created light, and separated it from the darkness (Genesis 1:1–5).
- **Day 2:** God created the atmosphere (vv. 6–8).
- **Day 3:** God separated the bodies of water, setting their boundaries and creating dry land. He filled the dry land with vegetation full of seeds to reproduce (vv. 9–13).
- **Day 4:** God set lights in the heavens to guide and keep time and seasons, separating day and night (vv. 14–19).
- **Day 5:** God filled the waters with creatures and the skies with birds, all capable of repopulating and filling the earth (vv. 20–23).
- **Day 6:** God created land-dwelling creatures. God then pivoted to create humankind as his companion. He gave humans dominion over the earth to look after and care for all he has made (vv. 24–31).

It is fair to say that God had a very busy six days. And then

- **Day 7:** God rested (2:2–3). And because man was with him and had not yet been given the important role of gardening and naming the animals, we can assume that man also rested with God.

We discover a pattern in this timeline: God worked, then rested, while man began with rest and then went to work. Watchman Nee, the late Chinese church leader and Bible teacher, made this observation:

The seventh day became the Sabbath of God; it was God's rest.

But what of Adam? Where did he stand in relation to that rest of God? Adam, we are told, was created on the sixth day. Clearly, then, he had no part in those first six days of work, for he came into being only at their end. God's seventh day was, in fact, Adam's first. Whereas God worked six days and then enjoyed his sabbath rest, Adam began his life with the Sabbath; for God works before he rests, while man must first enter into God's rest, and then alone can he work.[1]

Rest does not take away from our work but instead complements it. Picture a perennial, such as iris, peony, or lavender, sending up fresh, tender shoots as the ground thaws. In gardening, the best time to plant a perennial is in fall or early spring. This allows the plant time to restfully establish roots before the active growing season commences. Similarly, God calls us to begin with rest *before* we work. The Hebrew calendar reflects this beautifully. In Jesus's time and for those observing Hebrew traditions, a day begins at dusk. Thus, a day starts with rest. In traditional Hebrew observance, a weekly Sabbath (Shabbat) rest begins at sunset, with a full day of rest stretching until the sun sets on the following day. A day does not begin as early birds catch the worm or insects buzz about but rather when creation is settling down to rest . . . and inviting us to do likewise.

When we start with rest, we return to the pattern in Eden.

Don't worry right now about what day you will rest on—we'll get there later in our study. For now, focus on shifting how you think about rest. What is your mindset around work and rest? Do you work hard so you can enjoy the reward of rest? Challenge yourself to reframe your perception about where rest belongs. What are some ways you can rest before you engage in work each day and week?

## The Roots

> There remains a Sabbath rest for the people of God, for who-
> ever has entered God's rest has also rested from his works as
> God did from his. (Hebrews 4:9–10)

Sabbath rest | σαββατισμός | *sabbatismos* | sab-bat-is-mos' |
keeping Sabbath

In this particular passage, the practice of Sabbath rest is connected
to the perfect rest made available through Christ and has been de-
fined as "the blessed rest from toils and troubles looked for in the age
to come by the true worshippers of God and true Christians."[2]

Rested | καταπαύω | *katapauō* | kat-ap-ow'-o | cease, restrain

### Rest & Reflect

Following the patterns in Scripture, we'll return to the concept of
Sabbath throughout this study. But for now, record your immediate
reaction to and experience of observing the Sabbath.

### Under the Microscope

After forming Adam from the dust of the ground, we read in Genesis 2:15, "The LORD God took the man and put him in the garden

of Eden to work it and keep it." The word translated as *put*, נּיַח, or *yānah*, can also mean "rest," "settle down," and "give rest to." God settled Adam into a habitat where he could enjoy God's rest.

Is your tendency to rush into the work in front of you? Think of Adam resting with God before he set about his work in the garden. Consider your current workload and projects. How can you practice resting before working?

# WEEK 1

*Day 2*

# GOD CREATED REST
# FOR OUR PROVISION

HOUSE SPARROWS VISIT MY YARD every day, and it's likely they are in yours also. They are a cosmopolitan species, meaning they live in most geographic regions and on every continent except Antarctica. My favorite house sparrow fact is that the oldest fossil of one was discovered in a cave near Bethlehem, close to where Jesus was born. It is likely that Jesus grew up listening to their songs, like my kids are now. Consider, then, how he used birds in his teaching (including sparrows in Matthew 10). Although Matthew 6 doesn't mention a specific species, it's feasible that house sparrows were jumping around on the ground that day, scavenging for crumbs as he spoke these words in verse 26: "Look at the birds of the air: they neither sow nor reap nor gather into barns, and yet your heavenly Father feeds them. Are you not of more value than they?"

Feeding a house sparrow is no small undertaking. A house sparrow chick requires three to four thousand insects from when it hatches to when it fledges.[1]

Back at creation, God planned entire ecosystems with plants and insects to provide for the tiny house sparrow chicks. We are much more valuable to God than the birds, so we can trust that he has planned even more carefully for our needs. As he fashioned the skies, seas, dry land, forests, creatures, and birds, God wasn't only planning for our needs of food and water. He was planning to provide for us through rest, as we saw yesterday in the creation narrative.

The garden of Eden was teeming with bountiful provisions. Never since has there been a space so full of things pleasing to the eye, taste buds, nose, and stomach. *Eden* can be translated as "a place of pleasure" or "abundance." Many theologians and Bible scholars believe the garden of Eden was meant to spread and cover the earth, filling our planet with many colors, aromas, textures, and life. Eden was "a place of bounty, of gardens, of fruitful labor, and of freedom from fear or negative encounters with nature. Most importantly, it was a place where God himself rested and reigned."[2]

When God calls creation to rest, he is inviting it to partake of his provisions. And the more I observe and study nature, the more convinced I am that creation often obeys God better than we do.

Of course, because God created humans in his image and for a relationship with him, our obedience matters more to him than the loyalty of birds and trees. However, we can learn important lessons from creation's innate understanding of God's provision through rest and trust. When we peer into nature's designs, we can see the original engineering plans and how God carefully set up nature to thrive. Pastor and author Dave Williams said, "Watch the animals—they have rhythms, and they're instinctive. We have to choose to practice these things, but all of creation is created to have these rhythms of engagement and withdrawal, of labor and rest, and so I think if we pay attention, God can help us."[3]

Perhaps this is why, in Matthew 6, when Jesus tells the crowd not to be anxious about what they will eat or wear, he points their attention to the birds and flowers that rely on God's provision. As we explore the layers of rest in Scripture, we can simultaneously observe how the flow of nature is encompassed by God's tender care, which includes a time of rest, and we can do likewise.

One way God provides for nature is by giving it an instinct to rest, as we've already seen in hummingbirds and perennials. Rest is a vital activity in all of creation, including us. When we forgo rest, we are not only running ourselves to exhaustion but forfeiting one of God's primary provisions for us. As a part of God's original, perfect creation, rest was meant to meet us with peace and clarity. It keeps us from dialing up our lives to an unsustainable pace. It transfers us out of a domain of chaos and frenzy and centers us in God's presence, where we remember what matters most and where God would have us invest our time and energy. How often do we ask him to give us something we think we require? It makes no sense to ask him to care for our needs only to ignore his provision of rest. Consider what you have recently asked God for. Could his readily available supply of rest be an answer to that request?

### The Roots

> Thus said the Lord GOD, the Holy One of Israel,
> "In returning and rest you shall be saved;
>     in quietness and in trust shall be your strength."
>                                           (Isaiah 30:15)

Rest | נַחַת | *naḥaṯ* | nakh'-ath | quiet, calm, patience

Quietness | שָׁקַט | *šāqaṭ* | shaw-kat' | to be tranquil, at peace, and undisturbed

Trust | בִּטְחָה | *biṭḥâ* | bit-khaw' | trusting, confidence

## Rest & Reflect

In the Bible verse above, underline what rest is promised to provide. How might these help you confidently rest in God's provisions?

## Under the Microscope

Study the connection between rest and abundant provisions in Psalm 65:4–13 below. As you do, follow these steps:

- In verse 4, to *dwell* in God's courts can be translated as "rest." Write "rest" next to *dwell.*
- In verse 4, circle *satisfied,* which can be translated as "plenty," "enough," "full," and even "excess."
- In verses 10–12, circle *abundantly, bounty, overflow,* and *abundance.* Pay attention to how God provides abundantly for creation.

### PSALM 65:4-13

⁴ Blessed is the one you choose and bring near,
    to dwell in your courts!
We shall be satisfied with the goodness of your house,
    the holiness of your temple!

⁵ By awesome deeds you answer us with righteousness,
    O God of our salvation,

the hope of all the ends of the earth
and of the farthest seas;
6 the one who by his strength established the mountains,
being girded with might;
7 who stills the roaring of the seas,
the roaring of their waves,
the tumult of the peoples,
8 so that those who dwell at the ends of the earth are in awe
at your signs.
You make the going out of the morning and the evening to
shout for joy.

9 You visit the earth and water it;
you greatly enrich it;
the river of God is full of water;
you provide their grain,
for so you have prepared it.
10 You water its furrows abundantly,
settling its ridges,
softening it with showers,
and blessing its growth.
11 You crown the year with your bounty;
your wagon tracks overflow with abundance.
12 The pastures of the wilderness overflow,
the hills gird themselves with joy,
13 the meadows clothe themselves with flocks,
the valleys deck themselves with grain,
they shout and sing together for joy.

For further study, read Ephesians 1:3–20 and circle everything
that is ours through Christ.

As you take time to rest in God's presence, reflect on the fullness of his abundant provisions. How has he provided more than enough for you?

## WEEK 1

### Day 3

# GOD CREATED REST AS A GIFT

LIKE PERENNIALS, MANY CREATURES DEPEND on rest as a vital activity, and a disruption to this cycle of rest and work can be catastrophic, especially in the context of hibernation. Some mammals hibernate to survive cold months when food sources are limited. True hibernation normally involves an extreme (1) reduction in metabolism, (2) slowing of heart rate, (3) slowing of breathing, and (4) lowering of body temperature.

Fun fact: Bears don't hibernate. Although they go dormant and sleep for extended periods, their body temperatures only decrease by around ten degrees Fahrenheit, nowhere close enough to make them true hibernators. Their winter naps are called *denning* and are equally vital.

The woodchuck, also known as a groundhog, is a prime example of a true hibernating animal. During hibernation, it will lower its body temperature by about sixty-two degrees (from ninety-nine degrees Fahrenheit to thirty-seven). Compare that to humans, who will lose consciousness if their body temperature drops by a mere sixteen degrees. Not only that, but woodchucks reduce breaths per minute from around eighteen to two. Most extraordinarily, they slow their heart rates from eighty beats per minute to about five. God dialed in this incredible, highly integrated system for the survival of woodchucks and other hibernating animals. If their sleepy states are disrupted, they risk using all their energy reserves to raise their body temperatures at a time when food is scarce and those reserves cannot be replenished.

We are much the same. If we forgo or put off rest, we will quickly cease functioning properly. A disruption to our God-given cycles of rest can be catastrophic. God designed us with hormones, including melatonin, to signal our bodies when it's time to rest, and cortisol, to wake us. When we do not acknowledge and care for these systems, fatigue can overtake our bodies, minds, and spirits.

Rest is critical for all of God's creation. However, unlike plants, creatures, and us, God does not need rest. Isaiah 40:28 says, "Have you not known? Have you not heard? The LORD is the everlasting God, the Creator of the ends of the earth. He does not faint or grow weary; his understanding is unsearchable."

The Creator of the ends of the earth does not suffer burnout. So why did God rest on the seventh day? Quite simply, God rested because he wanted to.

Scripture tells us that he values rest and enjoys taking time to stop and delight in all he has made. He, in fact, enjoys spending time with you and me so much that he gives us the invitation to rest. You see, rest is not only a pattern and provision but a gift to delight in.

Regarding Shabbat rest, author and pastor John Mark Comer wrote, "The Hebrew word Shabbat means 'to stop.' But it can also be translated 'to delight.' It has this dual idea of stopping and also of joying in God and our lives in his world."[1]

God choreographed rhythms into creation to remind us to pause from our constant activity and take joy in what he has allowed us to accomplish. God didn't finish his flurry of work only to pass the baton on to Adam and rush into the next task. Instead, he intentionally rested. Can you envision what that first day of rest might have looked like? Do you think God introduced Adam to all creation's fragrances, colors, and textures? Perhaps that first exposure to the world inspired Adam's act of creativity: naming the animals.

For six days God's voice had set things into motion, and now he called for an abrupt stop. Indeed, he knew that after sin entered the world, humankind's propensity would be toward constant and unceasing activity. He knew you and I would prioritize what's urgent over what's important. And here, at the outset of history, he issued an all-important invitation: Before you begin your day's work, take joy in all you have accomplished.

Think about this for a moment. God set up a pattern of rest at the beginning of time. It is integral to the universe.

Yesterday we saw in Genesis 2:15 that when God placed (נָיַח, yānaḥ, "put," "rested") Adam in the garden, he planted the desire for purposeful work in his soul. Humanity was endowed with the life-giving work of cultivation. God's children were to carry on his work. He invited us to bring forth and nurture life. Shortly after, in Genesis 2:19, we see the second important responsibility given to Adam. "Now out of the ground the LORD God had formed every beast of the field and every bird of the heavens and brought them to the man to see what he would call them. And whatever the man called every living creature, that was its name."

Adam had a creative calling. It makes sense that the day he spent resting with God and delighting in creation served as inspiration for his work—and should do the same for ours. When we begin with rest and take time to delight in what God has made, our souls and work are better for it.

Creativity is involved in every field of work. When have you experienced a creative rut or block? When have you had a difficult time finding a creative solution to a problem? Is your tendency to try to muscle through that block and force a solution? The next time you're feeling sapped of inspiration or motivation, pause and pay attention to how God sparks new ideas in times of rest. Most importantly, take time to stop and delight in the process and what God is allowing you to accomplish.

### The Roots

> Stop and consider the wondrous works of God. (Job 37:14)

Stop | עָמַד | *āmaḏ* | aw-mad' | cease, take one's stand, remain, establish

Consider | בִּין | *bîn* | bene | show oneself attentive, consider diligently

Wondrous | פָּלָא | *pālā'* | paw-law' | marvelous, surpassing, extraordinary, difficult to understand

### Rest & Reflect

When we take time to stop and delight in what God has made, we gain a deeper understanding of his unfathomable ways. Take ten minutes to sit outside or look out your window and record the wonders of nature you observe. What do those wonders teach you about God's creativity, intelligence, and wisdom?

## Under the Microscope

Read Psalm 95:1–7 below. While you read, follow the steps below:

- Underline every mention of something God has made.
- Circle every word that reflects delight, such as *praise*, *sing*, *joyful*, and *worship*.

### PSALM 95:1–7

¹ Oh come, let us sing to the LORD;
    let us make a joyful noise to the rock of our salvation!
² Let us come into his presence with thanksgiving;
    let us make a joyful noise to him with songs of praise!
³ For the LORD is a great God,
    and a great King above all gods.
⁴ In his hand are the depths of the earth;
    the heights of the mountains are his also.
⁵ The sea is his, for he made it,
    and his hands formed the dry land.

⁶ Oh come, let us worship and bow down;
    let us kneel before the LORD, our Maker!
⁷ For he is our God,
    and we are the people of his pasture,
    and the sheep of his hand.

Look at your markings. How does God's creation compel us to delight and worship? How can you practice delighting in creation today?

## WEEK 1

### Day 4

# THE PATTERN OF REST
# WAS DISRUPTED

LAST SUMMER MY KIDS AND I discovered five monarch caterpillars in our milkweed patch. We brought them inside and carefully placed them into prepared glass jar habitats. Over the next week, we watched as the caterpillars ate constantly. When each was prompted by instinct, it ceased its activity, found a stick or surface to adhere a silk pad to, hung upside down in a J shape, and wrapped itself inside a chrysalis. Their tasks as caterpillars were complete, and it was time to rest before beginning their new work as butterflies. If at any point in the process their work or rest was disrupted, it would have been devastating. God designed rest to be life-giving and protective, and when those patterns of rest are upset, it can be deadly.

Shortly after God created rest as a pattern and gift, Satan set out to disrupt this design. Unfortunately, humankind settled for less than God's best. Adam and Eve caved to Satan's schemes and brought sin into God's perfect creation. Their decision affects our present reality, which includes a disrupted pattern of rest. When sin entered in, fulfilling endeavors took on pain and drudgery. Toil wrapped itself around our work like a thorny vine. God had formed Adam from the dirt and then called people to cultivate every living thing, with pauses to participate in God's perfect rest. Now, with sin introduced, the path to meaningful work has become tangled. We read the account in Genesis 3:17–19:

> Because you have listened to the voice of your wife
>> and have eaten of the tree
> of which I commanded you,
>> "You shall not eat of it,"
> cursed is the ground because of you;
>> in pain you shall eat of it all the days of your life;
> thorns and thistles it shall bring forth for you;
>> and you shall eat the plants of the field.
> By the sweat of your face
>> you shall eat bread,
> till you return to the ground,
>> for out of it you were taken;
> for you are dust,
>> and to dust you shall return.

I can see these outcomes where I live in Colorado. There are plots of land with soil so stripped of nutrients that only invasive weeds, thorns, and thistles grow. Restoring such land takes years, if not decades, of laborious work and intentional rest.

We might not work the land in a literal sense, but thorns and thistles wrap around our endeavors and pursuits. Our work as Christ followers, spouses, parents, friends, employees, business owners, and whatever other roles we take up are choked by Eden's curse.

Work and rest were bestowed as gifts before sin entered—work to give us purpose, and rest to refresh us and give us space to celebrate.

But sin's curse made work burdensome, and the ideal pattern of rest was broken.

The curse set in motion on Eden's soil spreads through creation like a disease. Like the landscape, our souls suffer the effects of a sin-struck world. We struggle to relate to God's pattern of rest or enjoy it as a provision and gift. And yet God's promise of rest remains. In nature we witness a sacred striving toward that rest. When trees release their leaves to autumn's breeze, or sunflowers follow the sun's descent below the horizon and bow until morning, we see a return to rest. Adam's sin and our inheritance of brokenness is overshadowed by a far greater legacy of redemption.

Romans 5:16–17 offers this hope: "The free gift is not like the result of that one man's sin. For the judgment following one trespass brought condemnation, but the free gift following many trespasses brought justification. For if, because of one man's trespass, death reigned through that one man, much more will those who receive the abundance of grace and the free gift of righteousness reign in life through the one man Jesus Christ."

When Adam and Eve sinned, death spread throughout the earth and mankind. This disruption affected God's original design of balance between work and rest.

But the Enemy doesn't get the final word. Restoration and life are available to us through Jesus Christ. Our relationship with God can be made new, and we can return to the pattern of rest and work established at creation.

Where can you see a disruption of rest in your own life? Have you had restful seasons that were jolted out of rhythm by trauma or hardship? Have you established a pattern of regular rest only to have it sidetracked by demands on your time? Trust that God can restore restful rhythms in your life no matter how far detached you feel from a restful reality. Ask him to bring new life as he helps you return to his pattern of rest and work.

*The Roots*

So that, as sin reigned in death, grace also might reign through righteousness leading to eternal life through Jesus Christ our Lord. (Romans 5:21)

Grace | χάρις | *charis* | khar'-ece | good will, loving-kindness, favor, bounty, delight

Reign | βασιλεύω | *basileuō* | bas-il-yoo'-o | rule, reign as king

*Rest & Reflect*

Jesus's shed blood restored what was broken in the garden. Although we still suffer the symptoms of sin here on earth, we can also take part in our inheritance in Christ. One aspect of rest is noticing the influence and reign of God's grace. How can you see God's loving-kindness and bounty in your life? What steps can you take to rest your mind in gratitude for the new life we have in Christ? Write down three things you're thankful for. Then find a piece of art, or print out a photo, that reminds you of God's grace and hang it where you will see it often.

*Under the Microscope*

What does it mean to enter God's rest? Read Hebrews 4:1–6 and reflect on the questions below.

## HEBREWS 4:1–6

¹ While the promise of entering his rest still stands, let us fear lest any of you should seem to have failed to reach it. ² For good news came to us just as to them, but the message they heard did not benefit them, because they were not united by faith with those who listened. ³ For we who have believed enter that rest, as he has said,

"As I swore in my wrath,
'They shall not enter my rest,'"

although his works were finished from the foundation of the world. ⁴ For he has somewhere spoken of the seventh day in this way: "And God rested on the seventh day from all his works." ⁵ And again in this passage he said,

"They shall not enter my rest."

⁶ Since therefore it remains for some to enter it, and those who formerly received the good news failed to enter because of disobedience.

- Rest is a promise, but does everyone obtain or reach it? (v. 1)
- Who enters God's rest? (v. 3)
- Why do some fail to enter God's rest? (v. 6)

In verse 6, some Bible translations use the word *disobedience*, which can also be translated as "unbelief." When we doubt God or his provisions, we're left restlessly grasping for what we think is best. As we lay doubt aside and take God at his word, we experience his rest. Is there an area of your life where you are struggling to trust

God? How can you practice relying on his provisions? Consider a few things that feel heavy or you find difficult to trust God with. Pray, "Lord, I'm resting this _____ in your hands. Now help me to rest in your presence."

## WEEK 1

*Day 5*

# GOD RESTORES US
# TO REST

SEEING CREATION DISRUPTED FROM REST is disconcerting. On day 3 we looked at how hibernating animals rest through winter. However, some animals brave the cold out in the open, and it's hard work. When heavy snow falls, I watch the animals around our neighborhood restlessly trying to survive. Deer nibble at shriveled olive branches while snow falls from the tree and covers their faces. Elk scavenge for the last apples clinging to branches. Rabbits brave a break in the weather to forage. Birds huddle in bushes, puffing up their feathers to keep warm. Wildlife works hard simply to make it through the cold months, waiting for spring's reprieve.

Unlike these animals, we do not need to wait for ideal conditions in order to find rest. God has already restored patterns of rest through Christ's redeeming work on the cross. No matter where life finds us, rest is available. Our task now is to practice

- living in God's pattern by resting before we work;
- relying on rest as God's provision for us and trusting him to meet our needs through it; and

- accepting God's gift of rest and viewing it not as a weakness but an opportunity to stop and delight.

What does it look like to be restored to God's rest? We don't know exactly what Adam and Eve's days in the garden looked like before they sinned. But we know this: For a blink of time, Adam and Eve experienced perfect fellowship with God, and it took place at nature's epicenter. While we can't return to Eden here on earth, we can step back into God's design of rest as we commune with our Creator and live in light of Christ's finished work.

Jesus came to earth to die in our place and rise to new life. His sacrifice restores us to future eternal rest. When we follow Christ, we fix our hope on the perfect rest we will one day have with God. No matter the situation in front of us, we can consciously and consistently return our thoughts to Christ, who offers security for our souls that no present situation can change. But we don't have to wait. Scripture says Jesus also restores our ability to have rest right now. We will explore the concepts of eternal rest and present rest next week.

Today, one way we can practically experience his original design of rest is by stepping outside.

Just after creation, we read in Genesis 3:8 that Adam and Eve "heard the sound of the Lord God walking in the garden in the cool of the day." Imagine if God took this stroll with Adam and Eve each day. Their relationship with God was centered around experiences in the natural world. Their conversations were complemented by birdsong and the gentle cascade of river water flowing around bends and between rocks. Like Adam and Eve's, our fellowship with God gains depth and breadth when we're out enjoying all he created. Structures and walls block out many sounds, aromas, colors, and activities of the outdoors. When we place ourselves in nature, our thoughts are naturally drawn to God's character and creativity. God designed nature to aid in this process of turning our thoughts to himself.

Have you ever experienced mental clarity while walking in the woods or next to a river? When God designed the universe and everything in it, he interconnected many facets of his creation. The late naturalist John Muir wrote, "When we try to pick out anything by itself, we find it hitched to everything else in the universe."[1]

A good example of this is how sounds in nature change our bodies and the way we think. Science is discovering how natural sounds—like birdsong, rainfall, or a bubbling brook—physically alter our bodies and brains. One study showed different mental and bodily responses when listening to natural sounds compared to artificial.[2] While artificial sounds drew participants' minds inward, to worries and anxieties, natural sounds lowered stress levels and pointed their thoughts externally and away from immediate problems. No wonder a walk in the woods does wonders for perspective.

Perhaps this is why, when Maltbie Davenport Babcock wrote his famous poem, "This Is My Father's World," he chose the word *rest* regarding thoughts about nature:

This is my Father's world:
I rest me in the thought
Of rocks, and trees, of skies and seas,
His hand the wonders wrought.[3]

What the Enemy tried to destroy in the garden has been restored by Jesus. We have full access to restful living for today and future eternal rest. Like Babcock, may we rest ourselves in thoughts of our Creator and all he has made for our delight. And may we, like Adam and Eve in those early days, enjoy a walk with God in the garden.

Practice resting your thoughts on God's designs. Choose a creature or plant and discover new insights into the fascinating ways God has designed it. Focus on how it rests. Engage your God-given curiosity, and allow your thoughts to be directed to everything lovely and true as you explore his fingerprints throughout creation.

## The Roots

> O LORD, how manifold are your works!
> In wisdom have you made them all;
> the earth is full of your creatures.
>
> (Psalm 104:24)

Manifold | רָבַב | *rāḇaḇ* | raw-bab' | many, more, abound

Wisdom | חָכְמָה | *ḥāḵmâ* | khok-maw' | prudence, technical skill

## Rest & Reflect

We cannot perceive the number of God's works in creation. Key inventions, including the telescope and microscope, opened our eyes to myriads of God's designs that, for thousands of years, went unperceived. We can only see so far into the universe, and even our own ocean floors have not yet been fully mapped. How much more might we yet discover? Yet every time we look intently at God's designs, we glimpse his supernatural wisdom. Adam and Eve enjoyed God's creation as they walked with him in the garden. Sit somewhere outside and then write down ways you can likewise rest your thoughts in God's wisdom and power as you consider his manifold works all around you.

### Under the Microscope

In theology there is a concept called the *already-not-yet kingdom*. It represents the idea that we are *already* saved (secure in Christ to spend eternity with God) but *not yet* fully experiencing the complete enjoyment of God's blessings. Put simply, we are a work in progress here on earth but hold to the hope we have in heaven. Consider these two realities applied to rest:

1. We are fully restored to eternal rest with God. We will one day spend eternity with him.
2. We are actively practicing living in God's rest here on earth. We are making the effort to step back into his pattern of rest as a provision and gift.

Acts 3:18–21 represents these two realities well. Read the passage below and use it to answer the questions.

## ACTS 3:18–21

[18] What God foretold by the mouth of all the prophets, that his Christ would suffer, he thus fulfilled. [19] Repent therefore, and turn back, that your sins may be blotted out, [20] that times of refreshing may come from the presence of the Lord, and that he may send the Christ appointed for you, Jesus, [21] whom heaven must receive until the time for restoring all the things about which God spoke by the mouth of his holy prophets long ago.

- What is required for our sins to be blotted out (for salvation and eternal rest)? What did Christ have to do (v. 18)? What is our responsibility (v. 19)?
- What does God's presence bring (v. 20)?

- What might "times of refreshing" look like? Can we experience God's refreshment now? How?
- What do you think it will be like when God restores all things? Will it be restful? What challenges to rest are you currently up against that will no longer be a reality?

# WEEK 1

## Days 6 and 7

# STOP & DELIGHT

*We will pause after each week to practice stopping and delighting in all God has made. This practice establishes a rhythm as we step back into cadence with creation. So whatever day "Stop & Delight" falls on, take time to practice biblical rest.*

## TAKE A WALK IN THE GARDEN

FIND A NATURAL SPACE AND go for a walk. This can be done in any season. Maybe you have a garden in your yard you can meander through or an arboretum in your town where you can enjoy a walk. Perhaps it's a trail through the trees or a stroll along the river. Begin your time by prayerfully casting your cares on Christ. Practice resting your mind on him. After you have placed your burdens in his hands, walk or sit silently. Attune your mind to the sounds, sights, and fragrances of creation. Sit or walk long enough that your thoughts unwind from present worries and naturally drift to God's provision and beauty. Take delight in the details of his creation.

### Journaling Questions

How might a rhythm of rest change your life?

What specifically do you need to regularly rest from? Media? Work? Service? Technology?

What are you asking God to provide in your current season? Could rest be part of his provision?

# WEEK 2

## ROOTS
## A Foundation of Rest

*Whoever has entered God's rest has also rested
from his works as God did from his.*

HEBREWS 4:10

*Day 1*

# THE ROOTS OF REST

EVERY AUTUMN, ASPEN TREES PAINT the Colorado mountainsides in vibrant hues of yellow, orange, and red. What strikes me is that these groves are not made up of individual, disconnected trees. An aspen grove is a single living organism. Each tree is actually a clone of the original tree and shares genetics and a root system. One such grove, called *Pando*, is one of the largest known living organisms (claiming second place to a honey fungus in the Pacific Northwest). Pando, Latin for "I spread," is estimated at over forty thousand individual trees with a shared root system spanning 106 acres in Utah. Each tree does not stand alone but in the company of others, vitally connected by shared roots.

There is a similar interconnectedness to the theme of rest in Scripture. Rest is not an isolated concept popping up here and there. Instead, it is a widespread root system. Like Pando's roots, rest spreads throughout the Bible as an underlying and foundational truth.

When seeds sprout beneath soil, they typically send an initial root downward. More roots quickly follow and spread. Last week we saw the first root of rest anchoring into the soil of Genesis, where God gave us a pattern of rest and work to follow.

This week we'll discover roots of rest spreading into the wilderness beneath the Israelites' feet and winding under Calvary hill, where Jesus made perfect rest possible. As we grasp the breadth of rest in Scripture, we discover its relevance and necessity. Like a healthy root system that stabilizes and nourishes a tree, rest is vital for our lives and faith. We will see how God's gift of rest rescues us from wandering, saves our souls, and transforms us to become more like Christ.

It is important to note that a primary passage we're studying this week, Hebrews chapters 3:7–4:11, primarily concerns salvation. Yet like a sprawling root system, it touches on rest in the Old Testament, New Testament, and for our daily lives. We will see how salvation in Christ—the ultimate and perfect rest—affects our daily lives and makes rest a reality.

It is noteworthy that God inspired the author of Hebrews to write in depth about salvation using the analogy of rest. His choice of metaphor places rest in a high-priority position—if something is as worthy of comparison with salvation, we should give it utmost importance.

As we explore the prominence of rest in God's Word, we have more context and confidence for accepting Jesus's invitation in Matthew 11:28–30:

> Come to me, all who labor and are heavy laden, and I will give you rest. Take my yoke upon you, and learn from me, for I am gentle and lowly in heart, and you will find rest for your souls. For my yoke is easy, and my burden is light.

Perhaps, like me, you find solace in Jesus's invitation: "Come to me . . . and you will find rest for your souls." Isn't soul rest what we are aching for? But maybe you also struggle to take him at his word. Is rest realistic in modern society?

Just as one tree does not stand alone, this Scripture is not an isolated mention of rest. Jesus's invitation and promise of rest is supported by the pervading theme of rest throughout Scripture, like a strong and sprawling root system.

We are quick to relate to the first part of the verse, as those who are heavy laden. Life is weighty. You may have wondered, like I have, if Jesus's measurements for weight are different from ours, because the latter part of the passage is hard to agree with. His yoke and burden often feel far from easy and light. Amid everything God has called us to, whether marriage, ministry, parenting, creating, career, serving, or all of those—whatever purposeful work he planted in our hearts—it can be difficult to believe the responsibility is anything but hard and heavy. But remember that Jesus's invitation in Matthew 11 does not stand on its own. It is supported by a vast root network spreading across the pages of Scripture, including his exclamation on the cross, "It is finished." His promise of rest for our souls in Matthew 11 is possible because of Jesus's finished work on the cross. Whenever we feel the work before us is too much, we can remember his words, "*It is finished*," and that the one who finished the work of our salvation is ready and at hand to help us in our work.

What aspects of your life feel heavy and restless? What is demanding energy beyond what you feel is available? Write it down in today's journaling space and ask God to help you lay it at the foot of the cross, where Jesus, who finished the work of our salvation, will meet you with sufficient help.

### The Roots

That Christ may dwell in your hearts through faith—that you, being rooted and grounded in love, may have strength to comprehend with all the saints what is the breadth and length and height and depth, and to know the love of Christ that surpasses knowledge, that you may be filled with all the fullness of God. (Ephesians 3:17–19)

Rooted | ῥιζόω | *rizoō* | hrid-zo'-o | to strengthen with roots, establish, cause a person or a thing to be thoroughly grounded

Grounded | θεμελιόω | *themelioō* | them-el-ee-o'-o | to lay the foundation, make stable, establish

### Rest & Reflect

In the prayer above for the Ephesian believers, the apostle Paul used the beautiful image of roots to speak to the breadth of Christ's love. As we comprehend more of Christ's love that surpasses knowledge, that love will wind through every area of our lives, creating a firm foundation beneath our feet and faith. How might God's gift of rest help you experience more of Christ's love? How might both his rest and love, working together, provide a nourishing and resilient root system to hold you up?

### Under the Microscope

Let's look closer at Ephesians 3. As you do, follow the steps below:

- Circle *rooted and grounded in love* in verse 17.
- Draw lines or arrows connecting *rooted and grounded*

in verse 17 to *strengthened with power* in verse 16 and *strength* in verse 18.

- Underline *the breadth and length and height and depth.* Write "roots" or draw roots next to these words. Whenever you read or hear this passage, think of Christ's love spreading like roots beneath you.

## EPHESIANS 3:14–19

[14] I bow my knees before the Father, [15] from whom every family in heaven and on earth is named, [16] that according to the riches of his glory he may grant you to be strengthened with power through his Spirit in your inner being, [17] so that Christ may dwell in your hearts through faith—that you, being rooted and grounded in love, [18] may have strength to comprehend with all the saints what is the breadth and length and height and depth, [19] and to know the love of Christ that surpasses knowledge, that you may be filled with all the fullness of God.

- In what areas do you need more strength? How can you allow Christ's love to permeate every area of your life?
- Think back to our study on perennial plant roots strengthening through rest. How might your faith and experience of Christ's love strengthen as you practice resting?

# WEEK 2

## *Day 2*

# REST FROM WANDERING

WANDERING CAN PROVE DEADLY FOR a migrating bird. Take, for example, the blackpoll warbler, whose migration journey is up to 12,400 miles long. Their impressive yearly trip includes a nonstop two- or three-day journey across more than two thousand miles of the Atlantic Ocean. This tiny songbird normally weighs only eleven grams—about the equivalent weight of two quarters placed into your palm. Before migration it will bulk up to around twice its normal weight—around four quarters, or 5 percent of a pound. There isn't much extra fat or energy to allow for side trips and off-track flying. The good news is that, besides the sheer endurance required to make such a journey, God equipped migrating birds with incredible navigation strategies.

Many scientists believe, and much evidence is pointing toward, a special Cry4 protein in some birds' eyes that helps them sense (perhaps even *see*) the magnetic field, which is invisible to us. Additionally, many birds are known to use the position of the sun during the day and stars at night to find their way. Of course, even with all the special tools and God-given equipment, birds still end up lost, which leads to a deadly expenditure of energy.

Wandering not only is dangerous to birds but also threatens our own pursuits of a restful life. God has a plan for how we move toward our destination. But we have a tendency to ignore special God-given tools and equipment (like the Bible, Holy Spirit, Christian community, and prayer) and go our own exhausting ways. You don't have to look far to observe the franticness of our society. Plotting our own path or trying to make our way in life leaves us depleted.

But what is it that initially compels us to wander away from God's best for what we think might be better? Doubting God's provisions and guidance has a lot to do with it, which was the case for the Israelites.

Hebrews 3:7–4:11 stretches its roots back to the promised land. Well, in the Israelites' case, *almost* to the promised land. God had rescued the Israelites out of slavery in Egypt and was leading them to a land that represented rest from their enemies and the blessing of God's abundant provisions. Yet doubt would keep them from entering God's rest.

Let's begin with Hebrews 3:7–11.

Therefore, as the Holy Spirit says,

"Today, if you hear his voice,
do not harden your hearts as in the rebellion,
on the day of testing in the wilderness,
where your fathers put me to the test
and saw my works for forty years.
Therefore I was provoked with that generation,
and said, 'They always go astray in their heart;
they have not known my ways.'
As I swore in my wrath,
'They shall not enter my rest.'

This passage refers to a pivotal point in the Israelites' journey, where they failed to remember God's faithfulness and were therefore prohibited from entering the promised land or experiencing its rest (Psalm 95:8–11). The Israelites had a habit of forgetting God's provisions and faithfulness. They figured they knew better than God, went astray, and often found themselves struggling as a result.

I know I've done this myself. Can you relate as well? When faced with an immediate need, we are hard-pressed to remember God's record of faithfulness, and we can find ourselves restlessly trying to provide for ourselves as we fly off course. In the Israelites' situation, their unwillingness to remember who God is and what he had done for them kept them from entering the promised land. Just as the Israelites experienced an amnesia of faith, our doubt can prevent us from partaking in God's promise of rest.

The promised land was rich in God's blessings, provisions, and rest, yet this generation of Israelites would never step foot on its soil because of their unbelief (Hebrews 3:19). Although our promised land might not be a physical location, we have God's blessings, provision, and rest available to us. As we accept these blessings from God's hand, we find rest from our wandering.

I recently explained this to a class of third- through fifth-grade students while teaching at our church. I told them that when I am struggling to trust God for the future, I make a list of all the ways he has been faithful and provided for me in the past. This practice allows me to rest in the assurance that God is taking care of my family. I don't need to wander aimlessly or exhaustively try to find or make my own way. Instead, I can stay the course by following Scripture and the Spirit and trust God for every step ahead. As I continue to do what I believe is right in light of God's Word, I am in constant prayer, making quiet space for God to tell me to make a course correction.

God's promise of rest is available to us—yes, right here. Right where you stand. In the whirlwind of life and all its demands, there is rest to be had—but it doesn't happen by chance. Instead, we experience rest as we bind our wandering hearts to God by trusting in him alone for everything we need. Don't waste precious energy by wandering away from God's course. Instead, experience his promise of rest as you reflect on his faithfulness in your life.

Let that grace now, like a fetter,
bind my wandering heart to thee.
Prone to wander, Lord, I feel it,
prone to leave the God I love;
here's my heart; O take and seal it;
seal it for thy courts above.[1]

In what ways has your heart wandered from God's rest? Ask him to bind your spirit to his promise of rest. Write down ways you are prone to wander, and commit those tendencies to God, asking him to seal your heart for his courts above.

### The Roots

We have come to share in Christ, if indeed we hold our original confidence firm to the end. (Hebrews 3:14)

Share | μέτοχος | *metochos* | met'-okh-os | partaker, fellow, partner (with other believers sharing in Christ's inheritance) (The same word is used in Hebrews 3:1 [NASB]: "Holy brothers and sisters, partakers of a heavenly calling, consider the Apostle and High Priest of our confession: Jesus.")

Confidence | ὑπόστασις | *hypostasis* | hoop-os'-tas-is | substance, that which has foundation, that which has actual existence

## *Rest & Reflect*

God's faithfulness provides substance to anchor our belief into. We are no longer a ship wandering or adrift at sea. As we reflect on God's past faithfulness, we have confidence to move forward and follow his leading. Make a list of ways God has been faithful to you in the past. When has he specifically provided for a need? Where has he given you direction? When has he brought encouragement?

## *Under the Microscope*

The passage we read in Hebrews 3 reflects back on Psalm 95 and is a reference to Meribah, where the Israelites wavered in unbelief and forgot God's past provisions. Verses 7–9 read,

> [7] Today, if you hear his voice,
> [8] do not harden your hearts, as at Meribah,
> as on the day at Massah in the wilderness,
> [9] when your fathers put me to the test
> and put me to the proof, though they had seen my work.

"My work" most likely refers to God's previous miraculous provisions when he held back the waters of the Red Sea for their escape from enemies and gave them food in the wilderness. However, in this passage, "my work" could be read in a broader context to include God's works seen in creation. The psalmist preceded this reference to the wilderness with verses 4–6:

⁴ In his hand are the depths of the earth;
    the heights of the mountains are his also.
⁵ The sea is his, for he made it,
    and his hands formed the dry land.

⁶ Oh come, let us worship and bow down;
    let us kneel before the LORD, our Maker!"

As we practice seeing God's works and how he provides for creation, we are better equipped to battle unbelief and rest in his promises. How might you commemorate what God has done for you this week or this month?

# WEEK 2

## Day 3

# ETERNAL REST

HUMANS HAVE LONG BEEN FASCINATED by the concept of immortality. We can see this in countless story plots. We can also glimpse it in a fascinating marine animal, the immortal jellyfish. Scientists are still uncertain about how long an immortal jellyfish can live. Jellyfish go through a life-cycle process, including turning from a juvenile polyp adhered to a hard surface in the sea to a free-floating medusa adult form. However, when an adult immortal jellyfish is injured or feels threatened, it can revert to its juvenile polyp form and begin the process of growing up all over again. Of course, the immortal jellyfish won't truly live forever, because the earth is temporary, and God will one day make a new heaven and earth (Revelation 21:1–5).

Perhaps humans are intrigued by the idea of immortality because God has placed eternity in our hearts (Ecclesiastes 3:11). We know there is more than what we see on earth. And maybe this longing for eternity directly correlates to our desire for rest. We understand there can be true, eternal rest with God. Unlike the immortal jellyfish who restlessly reverts to childhood and grows up time and again, we can look forward to the promised eternal rest of God.

From the first week of time, rest has pointed toward a perfect union with God, and after the fall, rest has pointed forward to salvation. We looked at the roots of rest reaching back to creation, where we saw God's perfect original design. We've also seen the theme of rest winding its way through the wilderness, where the Israelites' doubt kept them from experiencing God's gift. The roots of rest in the Old Testament press forward into the New Testament, where we find God's perfect rest restored through Jesus's death and resurrection.

Yesterday we read about the Israelites' wandering and rebellious hearts that kept them from physical rest in the promised land. The author of Hebrews opened chapter 3 by contrasting the leadership of Moses (who guided the Israelites in the wilderness) and Jesus (who leads us to perfect rest). Many Bibles contain a header for chapter 3 titled "Jesus Greater Than Moses." Of course, the contrast is intuitive. Moses was a great but flawed man. Jesus is God, who came to earth and put on flesh to save our souls, and while in human form, remained holy.

Still, the author of Hebrews does something beautiful here by comparing the leadership of Moses and Jesus before writing about rest. Under Moses's leadership, the Israelites never reached rest (the promised land). Jesus, on the other hand, brings us into perfect and eternal rest—his salvation (vv. 3 and 5–6).

Let's move into Hebrews 4:1–2 and notice the connection between rest and salvation: "While the promise of entering his *rest* still stands, let us fear lest any of you should seem to have failed to reach it. For *good news* came to us just as to them, but the message they heard did not benefit them, because they were not *united by faith* with those who listened" (emphasis added).

*Rest.*

*Good news.*

*United by faith.*

This rest-salvation connection becomes even clearer in verses 8–9: "For if Joshua had given them rest, *God would not have spoken of another day later on*. So then, there remains a Sabbath rest for the people of God" (emphasis added).

What does "if Joshua had given them rest" mean? This refers to when the Israelites, led by Joshua (Moses's successor), finally entered the promised land. Of course, those who had grumbled against God in unbelief never stepped foot on the promised land; their unbelief disqualified them. But verses 8–9 indicate that the promised land rest was only a beginning. It was a foreshadowing of a better rest to come. The roots of rest in Scripture were spreading wider and plunging deeper.

Joshua was able to bring the Israelites into the promised land, but he could not provide a permanent solution to bad choices and the gulf they create between us and the provider of perfect rest. The reality is that the promised land pointed to a more profound rest ahead: salvation rest, delivered not by Joshua but through Jesus Christ.

Jesus, as the Son of God, made perfect, eternal rest available by dying and rising to new life, giving us access to God and his gift of rest.

We can enjoy God's rest because Jesus's work of salvation is complete. When Jesus died on the cross to take our punishment, he declared, "It is finished" (John 19:30).

Because Jesus died in our place, we can cease striving to save ourselves (which is a futile endeavor). The only thing left is for us to accept God's offer of peace.

If you have accepted God's salvation rest, are you experiencing it daily? Are you living as a child redeemed, forgiven, and bought with the precious blood of Christ? Or do you struggle to trust God's acceptance and love? As we lay aside shame and recognize our worth in Christ, we can rest from tireless pursuits to gain his approval, because we already have it.

## *The Roots*

Whoever has entered God's rest has also rested from his works as God did from his. (Hebrews 4:10)

Rested | καταπαύω | *katapauō* | kat-ap-ow'-o | restrain, give rest, take rest, ceased

Works | ἔργον | *ergon* | er'-gon | anything accomplished by hand, art, industry, or mind

## *Rest & Reflect*

Ever since Adam and Eve hid from God in the garden of Eden, humanity has sought to cover up sin and shame. Often, even after turning from sin to follow Christ, we carry the weight of former failures and present struggles. In many ways, we are still attempting to cover up and hide, or to earn favor with God. Yet God makes it clear in this passage that we can cease this exhausting pursuit of self-righteousness and rest in Christ's finished work on the cross. Are past failures holding you back from experiencing God's acceptance and rest? Surrender those notions to God and ask him to replace shame, guilt, and self-effort with an increasing awareness of his righteousness and restful presence.

## Under the Microscope

Are you trying to work to please God? Or are you resting in his finished work on your behalf and experiencing his profound peace and acceptance? His salvation is sufficient. If you have never stepped into his salvation rest, do so today. Accept his gift of perfect, eternal rest.

> If you confess with your mouth that Jesus is Lord and believe in your heart that God raised him from the dead, you will be saved. For with the heart one believes and is justified, and with the mouth one confesses and is saved. (Romans 10:9–10)

If you have entered his perfect rest, ask him to help you experience his rest in your day-to-day living. Read Hebrews 4:8–10 alongside Isaiah 26:12 below.

| HEBREWS 4:8–10 | ISAIAH 26:12 |
|---|---|
| [8] For if Joshua had given them rest, God would not have spoken of another day later on. [9] So then, there remains a Sabbath rest for the people of God, [10] for whoever has entered God's rest has also rested from his works as God did from his. | [12] O Lord, you will ordain peace for us, for you have indeed done for us all our works. |

Who offers us perfect rest from our work? Write down how you might stop anxiously striving and instead take one step this week into God's gift of rest.

# WEEK 2

## Day 4

# TRANSFORMATIONAL REST

HAVE YOU EVER WATCHED A caterpillar wind up into its chrysalis or emerge as a butterfly? Last week when we learned about God's pattern of rest being disrupted, I shared about the monarch caterpillars our family reared. We had the privilege of watching three of the five caterpillars create their chrysalis and pop out as new butterflies (and if you've ever seen this process, it truly is a "popping out"!).

Inside the chrysalis, a caterpillar nearly completely liquefies itself, except for a few critical pieces, before re-forming into a butterfly. God designed caterpillars with a unique group of cells called *imaginal discs*, which form into the butterfly's new parts while inside the chrysalis. It's as if God tucked the imaginal discs into the caterpillar and said, "Just imagine what you'll become!"

Likewise, when God created us in his image, he gave us the potential to become like Christ. The process of becoming more like Christ is called *sanctification* and happens as we learn to live how Jesus lived.

As a young girl eager to follow Jesus, I tried my hardest to emulate the fruit of the Spirit in Galatians 5:22–23. *If only I can muster up more love, joy, peace, patience, kindness, goodness, faithfulness, gentleness, and self-control, then I can be more like Christ*—which is true, except I went astray right from the get-go by beginning with "if only I . . ." It is not I but Christ in me. If I try by my own means to become more like Christ, I am not operating in my image-of-God likeness but in a false view of self-righteousness.

Yesterday we saw that Christ finished the work of our salvation, so we have no need to work for access to God. Similarly, our efforts on their own do not make us more like Jesus. Like a caterpillar waiting in its chrysalis, we must wait and rest patiently as God does his continual, supernatural work in our hearts and minds. We get mixed up and frustrated when we try to become more like Christ through our strength and strategies, which are sorely limited. To force this transformation would be like a caterpillar deciding it had no time to rest in a chrysalis and instead attempting to rearrange itself into a butterfly on its own.

Sanctification comes only from God through Christ. Hebrews 13:12 says, "Jesus also suffered outside the gate in order to sanctify the people through his own blood." From this verse, who is it that sanctifies? Jesus Christ. By his blood, we are saved and secure. Also by his blood, we are being made more like him, which requires restfully depending on his transforming work in our hearts and minds.

After many failed attempts, I discovered that the way to sanctification is through the door of resting in what Christ has done, and that door is wide open.

Not that it is easy. Rest is a not-always-comfortable process meant to shape and form us into the image of Christ. It is a gift we can ask for and accept every morning, as Lamentations 3:22–24 reminds us:

The steadfast love of the LORD never ceases;
    his mercies never come to an end;
they are new every morning;
    great is your faithfulness.

"The LORD is my portion," says my soul,
"therefore I will hope in him."

God's new morning mercies include his gift of rest.

This connection between rest and becoming like Christ is a beautiful, cyclical process.

As you practice resting in Christ's finished work, you will become more like him. And, as you become more like him, you will better understand and experience his rest, which makes you desire to be more like him. Can you see the circle? Only it is not a flat circle. It's like a Slinky (if you were born after the nineties, maybe look up what a Slinky is). When outstretched vertically, the concentric circles continue on an upward path. This is what becoming more like Jesus looks like—a continuous path circling up to rest and into Christlikeness.

We can be confident that because God gave the greatest gift of his Son to secure our salvation, he will not withhold from us the gift of rest for our daily lives. Romans 8:32 offers this assurance: "He who did not spare his own Son but gave him up for us all, how will he not also with him graciously give us all things?"

Because God made eternal rest possible through salvation, we know he will also provide daily, experiential rest that transforms us to be more like Christ.

In what ways have you tried to force spiritual growth or take transformation into your own hands? Identify areas you desire to grow in, perhaps patience, love, kindness, or wisdom, and ask God to mature you in those areas, and to open your eyes to see him actively at work within you.

### The Roots

If anyone is in Christ, he is a new creation. The old has passed away; behold, the new has come. All this is from

God, who through Christ reconciled us to himself and gave us the ministry of reconciliation. (2 Corinthians 5:17–18)

New | καινός | *kainos* | kahee-nos' | recently made, fresh, unworn, of a new kind, unprecedented, novel, uncommon, unheard of

Reconciled | καταλλάσσω | *katallassō* | kat-al-las'-so | to receive one into favor (from ἀλλάσσω: to make different, change)

### Rest & Reflect

Notice the simplicity of this promise. It does not say, "If anyone is working for Christ" but instead "If anyone is *in* Christ." We will explore this truth more in week 6, "Abide." But for today, reflect on the promise that if you are in Christ, you are a new creation, and record ways he is actively making you new in your thoughts, actions, habits, and behaviors.

### Under the Microscope

Above, we placed the individual root words of 2 Corinthians 5:17, *new* and *reconciled*, under the microscope. Now, let's look closely at its poetics.

## 2 CORINTHIANS 5:17

<sup>17</sup> If anyone is in Christ, he is a new creation. The old has passed away; behold, the new has come. All this is from God, who through Christ reconciled us to himself and gave us the ministry of reconciliation.

In stunning imagery, the author, Paul, uses language from the creation narrative of Genesis 1–2. The word κτίσις (*ktisis*) is used for *creation*. It most often refers to the act of creation or what has been created. New Testament scholar Paul Barnett wrote this about the connection between 2 Corinthians 5:17 and Genesis 1–2:

> The apostle's use of the vocabulary of the creation narratives of Genesis is striking. It is implied that unbelievers (as Paul had been) are blind . . . and live in a darkness analogous to the primal darkness of the first verses of the book of Genesis. Just as God spoke then, and there was light, so too God now speaks the gospel-word and once again there is light, though it is inward within the heart. . . . As by the agency of the word of God the world was made, so now, by the word of God, the message of reconciliation, people are remade.[1]

*Rest* in God's work, for you are a new creation and also being made new day by day. Write down some ways God has transformed your ways of thinking or the desires in your heart. How is he making you more like Jesus? Then write a prayer asking for a specific way you would like him to transform or grow you.

# WEEK 2

## Day 5

# STRIVING TO REST

TREES DON'T SIMPLY DECIDE ONE chilly day to rest. They have a checklist of tasks to complete before they go dormant for winter. In a sense, they must work toward resting. In preparation for rest, they have to store food reserves in the form of sugars beneath their bark and in their roots. Then there is the problem of their leaves or, in conifer trees, needles, which they need to either shed or protect.

As forester and author Peter Wohlleben writes, "Shedding leaves is an active process, so the tree can't go to sleep yet." He explains that the tree pulls energy back from its leaves and stashes the reserves in its trunk. After that, "the tree grows a layer of cells that closes off the connection between the leaves and the branches."[1] This can be a cork layer where the leaf attaches to the branch. Think of this like having your yard sprinklers blown out in autumn. If a tree doesn't remove the water from its extremities and prevent more water from coming in through leaves, it might freeze and burst.

Deciduous (leafy) trees break down chlorophyll, the pigment that makes their leaves look green, which is why their true colors of yellow and orange show in autumn. In some trees, trapped sugars turn the leaves vibrant hues of red, purple, dark orange, pink, and even blue.

Evergreen trees (conifers that keep their needles year-round) have a different strategy, since they don't drop their needles. They pump a natural antifreeze into their needles to protect them throughout winter. Consider auto shops in late fall advertising antifreeze services for your car—trees must prepare similarly.

We can't simply decide to live a more restful life. In a world cursed by sin, the odds of falling into a restful life are not in our favor. Instead, we too must prepare and work toward rest.

This is why, to sum up his writing about rest, the author of Hebrews urged us in 4:11, "Let us therefore *strive* to enter that rest" (emphasis added). As we studied on day 3 of this week, the primary concern of this passage is salvation, and the author was encouraging readers not to delay in unbelief but to make haste to enter God's salvation so they could one day experience eternal rest. However, we can also apply this to striving toward rest in our daily experiences. We can work toward implementing restful habits, like pausing throughout our day to reflect on Scripture and pray. We can strive toward more restful days with margin carved out between activities. We can make the effort to wake a half hour early to rest in God's presence, or to put away devices in the evening for a peaceful close to a day. These practices require effort, but they reap the reward of more restful living, which is countercultural—we must make every effort to live by and in God's rest.

What is currently preventing you from enjoying God's rest? Is it an obsession with productivity? An addiction to distraction? An enslavement to worry? It's helpful to identify barriers so we can proactively create a life more conducive to God's rest. What might the challenges to rest be?

- A friend asking you to add an event or get-together to a day you've planned to rest?

- A work project taking more time than anticipated and a pressing deadline claiming your evening hours?
- A messy or cluttered house where it's impossible to feel restful?
- Notifications dinging on your phone?
- Sleeping too late and waking up already feeling behind on the day?
- A day's agenda tightly packed like a game of *Tetris*, so that when one appointment goes late or you hit all the red lights on your commute, your entire day (and attitude) is thrown off?

How could you remove some of these barriers? Could turning off notifications on apps, blocking out days or hours for rest, or leaving ten minutes early for appointments help protect you from these disruptions to rest? Again, rest takes effort and planning.

However, in Scripture we notice two distinct versions of striving—anxious and sacred. Anxious striving is described in Ecclesiastes 2:22–23: "What has a man from all the toil and striving of heart with which he toils beneath the sun? For all his days are full of sorrow, and his work is a vexation. Even in the night his heart does not rest. This also is vanity."

Does this vexation and vanity of work sound familiar? We often lapse into anxious striving because things need doing, bills have to be paid, our hearts do not rest, and we frantically run forward without heed for God's direction. Anxious striving leaves us restless, and there is only one remedy: God's rest, which we can access through sacred striving.

Sacred striving is far different from anxious striving. It is performed by God's power and accompanied by his peace. Consider these comparisons between anxious and sacred striving, and think about which one reflects your current reality.

| | |
|---|---|
| Anxious striving keeps you up at night. | Sacred striving is accompanied by God's indescribable peace. |
| Anxious striving depends on your efforts, energy, and grit. | Sacred striving depends on God's intervention and power—the same power that raised Christ from the dead: "What is the immeasurable greatness of his power toward us who believe, according to the working of his great might that he worked in Christ when he raised him from the dead and seated him at his right hand in the heavenly places" (Ephesians 1:19–20). |
| Anxious striving is driven by fear, comparison, and competition. | Sacred striving is focused on God's will and heavenly agenda above earthly possessions, preoccupations, or success. |
| Anxious striving says the outcome depends on you. | Sacred striving knows Christ has finished the work of salvation, is performing the work of sanctification, and is carrying out his plans and purposes through us. We can work faithfully, knowing God is the one who brings forth fruit: "I planted, Apollos watered, but God gave the growth. So neither he who plants nor he who waters is anything, but only God who gives the growth" (1 Corinthians 3:6–7). |
| Anxious striving is jaded by past failures and behaviors. | Sacred striving is infused with Christ's righteousness and gracious acceptance of us. |

Is your current reality and experience one of anxious or sacred striving? Look at the chart above and write your tendencies of anxious striving. Are you kept up at night thinking about tomorrow's demands? Are you relying on your grit to keep going? Are you driven by fear or comparison? Then write a prayer surrendering those tendencies and asking God to replace those responses or reactions with sacred striving. Ask him to help you focus on God's agenda and operate by God's intervention and power. Incorporate a prayer I recite nearly daily: *Lord, carry out this work at your pace, by your power, and for your glory.*

### The Roots

> One hand full of rest is better than two fists full of labor and striving after wind. (Ecclesiastes 4:6 NASB)

Rest | נַחַת | *naḥaṯ* | nakh'-ath | quietness, calm, patience

Labor | עָמָל | *āmāl* | aw-mawl' | misery, travail, sorrow, trouble, grievance

Striving | רְעוּת | *rᵊ'ûṯ* | reh-ooth' | vexation, longing

### Rest & Reflect

This verse certainly deals with anxious striving, as the Hebrew word for *striving* has also been translated as "vexation." Look also at the definitions for *labor*. This is not talking about the purposeful, God-fueled endeavors God created us for but rather the restless monotony of trivial pursuits. As we pursue God's rest, he'll align us with the work he created us for so we no longer spend our days striving after the wind, but instead live for his glory. Write down some of the life-giving work you feel God has called or is calling you to. Ask him to replace anxious striving with sacred striving and to bring work and rest into harmony in your life.

### Under the Microscope

Ephesians 2:8–10 puts work and rest in their rightful places—under the umbrella of sacred striving in God's power. Read the passage below and follow these steps:

- Circle *not as a result of works* and *for good works.*
- Underline *we are his workmanship.*

## EPHESIANS 2:8-10

[8] For by grace you have been saved through faith. And this is not your own doing; it is the gift of God, [9] not a result of works, so that no one may boast. [10] For we are his workmanship, created in Christ Jesus for good works, which God prepared beforehand, that we should walk in them.

Now consider how work is portrayed. We are God's work. We are created for work that he planned out long ago. Our salvation and acceptance does not come through that work. Instead, because God has saved us, we are qualified and equipped for the work. Performing the tasks God has in mind for us is sacred striving.

What are one or two tasks or jobs you believe God has called you to? How might knowing God created you especially for this work help you rest as you trust his plan?

# WEEK 2

*Days 6 and 7*

# STOP & DELIGHT

## REST ON EVERY SIDE

THIS WEEK, WE SAW HOW the Israelites' unbelief in the wilderness kept them out of the promised land. Eventually, under Joshua's rule, they entered the physical promised land of rest, albeit a temporary respite, looking forward to the ultimate rest available in Christ. Let's watch the scene unfold in Joshua 21:43–45:

> The LORD gave to Israel all the land that he swore to give to their fathers. And they took possession of it, and they settled there. And the LORD gave them rest on every side just as he had sworn to their fathers. Not one of all their enemies had withstood them, for the LORD had given all their enemies into their hands. Not one word of all the good promises that the LORD had made to the house of Israel had failed; all came to pass.

Take a walk and ask God to give you "rest on every side." Look for perennial plants and enjoy their beauty, which only comes after seasonally resting their roots. Look for butterflies and think about their restful time in the chrysalis, waiting for transformation and growth. Notice the trees. Are their leaves vibrant green after resting in winter? Are they turning colors, preparing to rest? Or are they dormant, waiting to put out new leaves after resting? Name specific areas of unrest or attack that you most need his presence to touch. Then stop and delight, giving him thanks for all his promises that have come to pass—including his promise of rest.

## Journaling Questions

Are your thoughts or affections wandering from God's course? Are you wasting energy, chasing after the wind or anxiously striving for something God doesn't want for you?

Are you working to earn favor with God? Take time to thank him for his acceptance and unconditional love.

What makes you feel restless or exhausted? Your calendar? Email or text notifications? Expectations from yourself or others? Prayerfully ask God to help you surrender what is draining and invite him to transform you through his gift of rest.

# WEEK 3

## WAIT
## An Invitation to Rest

*They who wait for the LORD shall renew their strength;*
*they shall mount up with wings like eagles;*
*they shall run and not be weary;*
*they shall walk and not faint.*

ISAIAH 40:31

# WEEK 3

## Day 1

# WAIT AND HOPE

FAIRY SHRIMP MIGHT BE ONE of the best examples we find in nature of waiting.

One afternoon while climbing boulders in the Rocky Mountains, my sons discovered vernal pools—tiny pond systems—in the depressions of the massive rocks. Upon closer inspection, they noticed several different living organisms in the water, including fairy shrimp—a freshwater shrimp.

Fairy shrimp lay their eggs in seasonal vernal ponds. After the females die, the eggs remain dormant in the dried-up ponds until water returns. That is when the eggs hatch and a new generation of fairy shrimp emerges.

In some cases, when water is in short supply and the temporary ponds don't refill, the eggs can survive dormant for years, possibly even decades or centuries. When rain finally arrives, the eggs burst into life. We are well familiar with drought seasons in Colorado, and it was likely the depressions we found had been dry for years. I wondered how long the fairy shrimp my sons found had waited to hatch.

Fairy shrimp live and reproduce in a highly unpredictable environment. They are a beautiful reminder that we must let go of control and allow God to arrange the circumstances around us as we wait on his timing.

What seasons of waiting have you endured?

Perhaps you are walking through one now. Maybe *walking* seems a lousy term for what you're experiencing, because times of waiting often feel painfully idle, maybe even useless. Yet God can make much of life's moments, including those spent waiting. He wants to use these slow-moving life chapters to impart a restful confidence in his sovereignty, plan, and power.

Isaiah 40:31 (NIV) says, "Those who *hope* in the LORD will renew their strength" (emphasis added). There seems to be a big difference between *wait for* the Lord in the English Standard Version and *hope in* the Lord in the New International Version. But the word used here, *qāvâ* (קָוָה) (pronounced kaw-vaw'), means to both "wait" and "hope" simultaneously. It is essentially its own verb. There is no English equivalent. So translators place it in a box of either hope or wait. But the original language tells us to wait with hope, or more accurately, to wait with great expectation. While the English word *wait* often communicates a ceasing of activity or idleness, *qāvâ* doesn't carry such connotation. It is an invitation out of restlessness.

Parents often feel restless in the weeks after they bring a newborn baby home, when sleep is hard to come by. However, with our fourth child, it was the weeks preceding her birth that left me restless.

I went in for a routine checkup at thirty-three weeks pregnant and found myself admitted to the hospital with a fetal heart-rate monitor strapped tightly around my stomach. A machine etched patterns of our daughter's heart beat onto a paper scroll. Every few minutes, a nurse came in to note any changes, of which there were none.

My doctor explained that the nonstress test was nonreactive. Our baby was not showing any accels in heartbeats. Her heart was certainly beating, but in an abnormally calm state, without the expected change of pace an infant's heart should show. We were monitored throughout the night, nurses in scrubs in case we needed an emergency C-section. They explained that should they need to take her out during the night, she would immediately be flown to a nearby hospital with a NICU. I was given a steroid shot to rush the growth of her lungs in case she needed to take her first breath nearly two months early.

In the morning my doctor explained she still had no idea what was causing the abnormal heart activity, but things seemed stable, and we were allowed to return home. She wrote up an intensive monitoring schedule of two to three doctor visits each week.

Returning home, I didn't know whether to feel relieved my daughter could keep growing inside me or terrified because I couldn't control the unknown circumstances in my womb. Sleep was elusive over the following weeks, as I stayed up through the night counting her kicks. At nearly thirty-seven weeks, when my amniotic fluid ran out, my doctor induced labor. The following day, with snow cascading out the hospital window, we held our first and only daughter after three sons. She was hardly five pounds, yet her tiny frame felt like the weight of a miracle in my arms.

As the nurses checked her over, I braced for difficult news. What would they find as the cause of all our angst? And yet our daughter was perfectly fine. Her heart, which had caused so much restlessness, was intact and beating strong.

Throughout the month before her birth, God was strengthening my ability to wait well. Reflecting on those weeks, I realize I definitely wasn't good at resting in God. But now, six years later, I look back and can see his gentleness and power surrounding that season of waiting. What I saw as restless and unnecessary was the channel through which he was deepening my faith in his sovereignty. I couldn't rely on myself or the doctors to calm my fears or save my daughter. God was drawing me into a more profound and unworldly trust and assurance.

Saint Augustine once wrote, "Our hearts are restless until they rest in You."[1] Worldly forms of respite and reprieve—even good ones—are not ultimately satisfying. Only in Christ's person and presence can we find soul rest.

What makes you feel restless right now? Is it an unknown future, a desired outcome, frantic living, or anxiety? Our restless condition will progress and infect our perspective and behavior. The cure to restlessness is not found in a perfectly polished agenda, vacation time, work schedule, or answers to life's questions. So how do we rest and renew our strength? We wait expectantly, remembering God's past faithfulness in our lives and praying in line with his promises in Scripture. We acknowledge the outcome might not be exactly what we are envisioning, but we ask for his intervention and provision and for him to act for our good and his glory. We choose to believe God is never late but is instead working according to his perfect timeline. We can say out loud, "God never fails." Look for proof in nature and in our past that God never turns his attention away from us. We can remind ourselves that he is present and active, and we can wait with excited expectation for how he will come through.

How is God calling you to *qāvâ* (wait with expectation) right now? What unanswered questions are causing angst? Where do you feel restless? Don't allow seasons of waiting to pass without imparting to you their faith lessons. These times are the fertile soil where God plants seeds of confident faith. Believe that God will help you rest in his faithfulness and see your strength renewed.

### The Roots

> Lead me in your truth and teach me,
>> for you are the God of my salvation;
>> for you I wait [*qāvâ*] all the day long.
> (Psalm 25:5)

Lead | דָּרַךְ | *dārak* | daw-rak' | guide

Teach | לָמַד | *lāmad* | law-mad' | instruct, expert, diligence, skill

Wait | קָוֶה | *qāvâ* | kaw-vaw' | look for, expect

## Rest & Reflect

Here, we see *qāvâ* beautifully paired with God's actions. As we, like the psalmist, wait all the day long, God is actively leading and teaching us. Waiting, then, is full of activity and movement, if not on our part, on God's. We do not need to be frustrated when we seem to be stuck, forgotten, or sidelined. In our waiting, we can actively seek and receive truth and wisdom from God. Consider how you can practically "wait all the day long." Write ideas below. Perhaps begin your day by writing out situations you're watching for God to act in, or pausing several times throughout the day to notice God at work in your mind, heart, or circumstances.

## Under the Microscope

Isaiah 55:10–11 uses the beautiful imagery of rain and snow watering the earth to communicate the effectiveness and hope of God's Word. A seed lays dormant in the ground until moisture coaxes it open. Similarly, his Word refreshes our spirits, awakening seeds of truth and goodness to sprout, grow, and flourish in his good time. Read the text and follow the steps below, then consider the questions after:

- The Hebrew word for water is רָוָה (*rāvâ*). Circle *water* and write these definitions next to it: "fill, satisfy, saturate."
- Draw a line or arrow connecting *rain, snow,* and *word.*
- Draw a line connecting *bring forth and sprout, accomplish,* and *succeed.*

## ISAIAH 55:10–11

[10] For as the rain and the snow come down from heaven
and do not return there but water the earth,
making it bring forth and sprout,
giving seed to the sower and bread to the eater,
[11] so shall my word be that goes out from my mouth;
it shall not return to me empty,
but it shall accomplish that which I purpose,
and shall succeed in the thing for which I sent it.

- From this analogy of rain and water, does it seem that the results of God's Word are always immediate? When have you seen God take time to grow a seed of truth or fulfill a promise in your heart or someone you know?
- What truth or promise has God recently impressed on your heart? Ask him to water that seed and cause it to flourish and bring new life in his perfect timing. Ask him to help you wait well in this beautiful process.

# WEEK 3

*Day 2*

# WITHDRAW TO A QUIET PLACE

WHEN YOU THINK OF A busy insect, what comes to mind? Bees have a reputation for being constantly active, hence the term "busy bee." Yet bees' sophisticated system of making honey depends heavily on rest.

My mom is a beekeeper, and she shared that bees require five to eight hours of sleep a night and need adequate rest periods to yield a good honey crop. One experiment found that sleep deprivation negatively impacts a honeybee's "waggle dance." Bees perform this waggle dance to communicate to their hive mates what direction and how far a good pollen source is located. It seems when a bee is tired, it cannot communicate as well, meaning less efficient pollen gathering and honey production. Even busy bees follow God's pattern of resting and working, which is a rhythm Jesus continued during his time on earth.

Jesus had a three-year ministry. Luke 3:23 starts the clock: "Jesus, when he began his ministry, was about thirty years of age." The timer goes off about three years later when Jesus ascended into heaven. This included what must have been an incredible forty-day epilogue after Jesus rose from the dead and remained on earth, providing eyewitness proof of his existence and victory over death (Acts 1:1–3). During his ministry, Jesus was exceptionally busy. In fact, Scripture doesn't even detail everything he was working on. John 21:25 says, "Now there are also *many other things* that Jesus did. Were every one of them to be written, I suppose that the world itself could not contain the books that would be written" (emphasis added).

The miracles the disciples focused on when recording the gospel books were not Jesus's complete repertoire. The accounts they told were carefully selected by God to carry a narrative throughout Scripture. They point back to the prophecies that foreshadow Christ's assignment, fulfill that rescue plan, bring us in on the mission, and direct our attention to an everlasting kingdom.

But there was more.

"Many other things that Jesus did."

Can you imagine?

If you are a mother or in a role of serving others, you might relate to this passage. Are there *many other things* you do on a daily basis that are never recognized by those around you? Unseen responsibilities demand time and energy, but they do not need to (and shouldn't) deplete you. But what can defend you against exhaustion? Let's look at how Jesus went about resting, waiting, and working.

Jesus was busy during those three years of ministry, much busier than even the gospel accounts portray. And yet, amid his responsibilities and the pressing, urgent needs of the masses, we see a habit holding him up. He did not rush from one miracle to the next. Instead, his busy years of ministry were punctuated by waiting.

Jesus sought out silence and solitude.

He regularly withdrew to quiet places.

He stepped back from people, events, and tasks to gain perspective and commune with his father. This is how he oriented himself while on earth.

We can follow Jesus's example and create habits of regularly withdrawing from the noise of the world. We can accept his invitation in Mark 6:31: "Come with me by yourselves to a quiet place and get some rest" (NIV).

When we spend time with Jesus, his inclination toward silence and solitude seeps into us.

What is your quiet place? Spend a moment with that question. Picture it in your mind. Is it hazy? Disrupted? Nonexistent? Or does it come right to mind? Is it regular or inconsistent?

A closet?

An hour of the morning before the sun rises along with the day's demands?

A walk at lunchtime?

A commute with worship music?

A hike or run through the woods?

To Jesus, rest and quiet were nonnegotiable. Do we take seriously Jesus's invitation to enjoy silence and solitude? Do we see rest and waiting as vital activities?

We are not meant to live as busy bees hurriedly rushing from one activity to the next, but to emulate the pattern we find in creation and in Jesus's life of resting, waiting, and working. Take time today to withdraw from constant activity and follow Jesus to a quiet place.

### The Roots

> Come with me by yourselves to a quiet place and get some rest. (Mark 6:31 NIV)

> Quiet | ἔρημος | *erēmos* | er'-ay-mos | solitary, desolate, wilderness

Rest | ἀναπαύω | *anapauō* | an-ap-ow'-o | refresh, take rest, give rest

## Rest & Reflect

Jesus spoke that beautiful invitation to his disciples immediately following a flurry of ministry activity. There is no doubt they were weary. His words travel like a ripple in the water over two thousand years and reach us today: Go with him to a quiet place and get some rest.

When has God refreshed you after a busy season? Reflect on times of an intense work or mental load. Look carefully to identify how God restored you physically, mentally, and spiritually. If you are currently in a busy season, ask God to prepare you for restoration. Make sure you have a plan in place so the intense season has an end in mind, and space for rest after.

## Under the Microscope

Yesterday we saw the connection between waiting and hoping in Isaiah 40:31. Psalm 62:5 makes a similar statement: "For God alone, O my soul, wait in silence, for my hope is from him." *Wait* in silence. My *hope* is in him.

The Hebrew word in this verse for *wait* is דָּמַם, or *dāmam*. It means "to cease," "lean in here," "be silent." The same word is used elsewhere in Scripture and translated as "be still." To be still is not only a cessation of activity but a settling into trust that quiets our souls.

How will you pursue silence this week? Consider one of the following:

- Turn off notifications on your phone and laptop.
- Delete a social media app for the week.
- Set an away message on your email for a day or two and don't check messages.
- Take a walk by yourself without music or headphones.
- Light a candle and spend five or ten minutes in silence to begin your day.
- Choose to count to ten before answering a frustrating question or dilemma.
- Take a nap in a hammock.
- Bring a camera to your favorite park and photograph God's wonder. If you have children, involve them in exploring and finding God's beautiful designs in nature.
- Write a poem, prayer, or a few thoughts about God's creation.
- Involve your children—encourage them in the practice of silence as well. Sit outside in nature and challenge them to be silent for a full minute and to simply listen. After a minute, ask them what they heard.

# WEEK 3

*Day 3*

# WAIT FOR PERSPECTIVE

WHEN WE THINK ABOUT POLLUTION in the ocean, our thoughts are often drawn to plastic water bottles on beaches or large "trash islands" floating on currents. However, there is another type of pollution that negatively effects marine animals: noise pollution. This is any unnatural sound that disturbs an animal's normal behavior, such as whales and dolphins using echolocation to locate and communicate with others of their species. Noise from shipping, military sonar, seismic blasts, and machines for exploration can confuse marine animals that depend heavily on sound vibrations to hunt, navigate, and communicate.

Excess and unnatural noise have negative effects on us also. They undoubtedly steal our peace and perspective and can harm our mental health. Whether audible sounds from devices, traffic, and modern life or abstract noise in our minds from tasks, responsibilities, and stress, noise can deafen us to God's voice and drown out his sacred perspective. I experience this when unanswered emails in my inbox steal my focus and distract me from what God has asked me to do that day. Or when the buzz of a notification on my phone jolts my attention away from the conversation in front of me to a nagging curiosity of what might be on my phone. What noise or distractions hijack your focus?

Yesterday we saw how Jesus's habit of withdrawing to a quiet place kept him grounded amid busyness. Today let's consider how this practice of waiting in a quiet place gave him perspective and can do the same for us.

Waiting is not often by choice. Instead, we find ourselves somewhat reluctantly (perhaps a tad bitterly) enduring in-between seasons. Maybe you are waiting on an answer to prayer or direction for a decision. Maybe you're waiting for provisions or a go-ahead for a dream or idea. Perhaps you're waiting for physical healing or the restoration of a relationship. Waiting is uncomfortable and can feel futile, as if we're forced into it. And yet in looking at Jesus's life, we see him *choosing* to wait.

Divine power fueled Jesus's heavenly assignment, but he still subjected himself to human limits and felt what we feel. He was God and man. What sustained him? The answer to that question will provide solutions to our challenges of faithfully carrying out kingdom work. The first chapter of Mark gives a beautiful example.

Mark 1 portrays a whirlwind of activity. The opening scene centers on John the Baptist's ministry and Jesus's baptism. Before the chapter closes, Jesus had achieved many successes. He

- spent forty days in the wilderness and endured the human experience of temptation;
- began his preaching ministry in Galilee;
- called his first four disciples (started a movement);
- taught in Capernaum (on the Sabbath of all days, radically marking himself as one with authority—even more than the regular Sabbath teachers);
- cleansed a man of a demon;
- became famous ("And at once his fame spread everywhere throughout all the surrounding region of Galilee" Mark 1:28); and

- healed "many" people who were sick, and cast out "many" demons.

All in the first thirty-four verses.

And remember from John 21:25 the "many other things that Jesus did."

Anyone today would look at such a budding minister and warn of impending burnout. *He won't last. His methods and growth are unsustainable. He'll give up ministry. He'll have a moral failing. He must have a vice.*

Jesus had no vices.

He never failed.

He did not burn out (eternal light never does).

What was his secret?

When the society around him grew loud with needs, accusations, and questions, how did he stay focused on God's plan?

What did he lean on? What can we lean on when overwhelm shrouds our vision?

We see it in Mark 1:35: "And rising very early in the morning, while it was still dark, he departed and went out to a desolate place, and there he prayed." The Greek word translated as "desolate" is *erēmos*. We saw it at the end of yesterday's reading when we looked at Mark 6:31. It can be translated as "desolate," "quiet," or "wilderness." Chapter 1 verse 35 is a hard stop between activities. Immediately after this, Jesus returned to teaching all throughout Galilee and casting out demons. But verses 36–38 show us the power of his pause:

> Simon and those who were with him searched for him, and they found him and said to him, "Everyone is looking for you." And he said to them, "Let us go on to the next towns, that I may preach there also, for that is why I came out."

The city was a flurry of activity. Excitement was brewing for this new teacher. Jesus had gone viral. The crowds were growing louder. But where was this celebrity everyone was talking about? "Everyone is looking for you," the people said. I picture a well-known pastor who cannot be located at a major event. The countdown timer on the screen has been at 00:00 for several minutes. The stage is empty, and the audience awkwardly squirms. He's in a back room, praying for those he'll impact.

This was Jesus's way.

We are not told that Jesus explained himself to Simon and the others. Instead, he offered this abrupt and confident response: "Let us go on to the next towns, that I may preach there also, for that is why I came out."

Jesus's pause gave him perspective. He chose to wait, which was how he oriented himself within his human experience. His communion with the Father kept him fiercely focused on the mission. Jesus's example gives us permission to pull away from the crowds, noise, and even responsibilities to rest and gain perspective.

He knew his purpose: "That is why I came out."

If ever you're confused about what to do next, go to *erēmos*—the quiet place, the wilderness—and get with the Father. Take a sacred pause and gain perspective for the way ahead.

### The Roots

The creation waits with eager longing for the revealing of the sons of God. (Romans 8:19)

Waits | ἀπεκδέχομαι | *apekdechomai* | ap-ek-dekh'-om-ahee | expect fully, look for

Eager longing | ἀποκαραδοκία | *apokaradokia* | ap-ok-ar-ad-ok-ee'-ah | anxious and persistent expectation

## Rest & Reflect

We might walk into a calm forest like we envisioned yesterday, a quiet place or wilderness, and think all is still and silent. However, there is steady and consistent activity taking place. Creation itself is waiting. It fully expects and looks forward to the Creator's making all things new. What if you and I learn this lesson and adopt this expectant longing as we spend time in *erēmos*, the quiet place? Like creation's, our waiting should not be idle. If we persistently look for and expect God to make all things new, God will grant us fresh perspective. In what ways do you need God to make something new? What needs to be restored? Write a prayer below asking him for renewal and to help you wait on his perfect timing.

## Under the Microscope

Withdrawing into solitude with his Father was a constant pattern in Jesus's life. It's a beautiful reflection of the pattern of rest and work God set forth at creation. Let's look at Jesus's rhythm of life as you read the Scriptures below.

- Luke 5:15–16
- Luke 6:12
- Mark 1:35
- Matthew 14:23

In light of these verses, answer the following questions:

- What was Jesus's response to noise and acclaim?
- Where do you feel the pressure to perform or meet expectations?
- How might you practice pausing for perspective when life gets busy?
- What did Jesus always do when he withdrew to quiet places? How can you make prayerful pauses a regular habit? Consider setting an alarm on your phone to pause for five minutes a few times throughout your day. Regroup your thoughts and attention during that time by asking yourself what you're currently busy with and if it's a worthwhile use of your time. Consider anything that is causing stress or tension, and ask God—audibly, in your mind, or on paper—to give clarity in those areas. Prayerfully ask him to melt away any overwhelm and replace it with confidence and delight.

# WEEK 3

## *Day 4*

# WAITING IN PREPARATION

ON THE FIRST DAY OF this week, we learned how fairy shrimp eggs wait for the right outside conditions to hatch. We find a similar waiting in lodgepole pine tree seeds.

Lodgepole pine seeds are enclosed and protected by *serotinous* pine cones, which are sealed shut with resin. Serotiny refers to seeds or cones that can wait for years until the right conditions cause them to open. If the cones fell to the ground, opened, and germinated, the seeds would be vulnerable to animals and fungi. The seeds also face difficulty making it into the soil if there is a lot of old underbrush like sticks and pine needles covering the forest floor. Their best opportunity to germinate is after a wildfire, which clears the underbrush, melts the protective resin coating, and creates an environment suitable for fresh growth. The lodgepole seeds, now released from their cones, fall into rich soil and take root.

The lodgepole seeds must restfully wait for the optimal conditions before they can continue their God-given initiative to grow and thrive. Sometimes God calls us to similar seasons, in which we're sealed shut and then sent through the fire before we can carry on the work he has called us to. In fact, waiting can be an essential piece of our work, because God is far more interested in performing work *within* us than watching the work he does through us.

Has God ever revealed a new path for you and then called you to wait? If you're like me, once God tucks an idea in your mind or purpose in your heart, you're eager to begin. In recent years, God has been training me to place a pause between his revelation and my action so I can sit with what he has revealed through his Word or Spirit before I do anything.

Maybe you relate to my inclination to rush into an endeavor. Or perhaps you're more prone to hesitate, maybe even overthink, before settling into decision fatigue. Whatever your response when God nudges you toward his plan, you can find wisdom in the apostle Paul's story and permission to engage in a restful pause before moving forward.

Like Jesus, Paul did not rush ministry. In Galatians 1:11–21, we glimpse Paul's life following his miraculous conversion. We learn that God revealed himself to Paul and called him to share the gospel message with many. However, Paul did not immediately begin preaching. Read verses 15–21 below.

- Underline the things Paul did *not* do.
- Circle how many years he spent waiting.

When he who had set me apart before I was born, and who called me by his grace, was pleased to reveal his Son to me, in order that I might preach him among the Gentiles, I did not immediately consult with anyone; nor did I go up to Jerusalem to those who were apostles before me, but I went away into Arabia, and returned again to Damascus.

Then after three years I went up to Jerusalem to visit Cephas and remained with him fifteen days. But I saw none of the other apostles except James the Lord's brother. (In what I am writing to you, before God, I do not lie!) Then I went into the regions of Syria and Cilicia.

Did you catch that?

*Then after three years . . .*

Have you ever held a dream or idea for years? My husband and I are both entrepreneurs. Ideas come quickly and abundantly, and they demand attention. They are like a five-dollar bill or piece of candy burning in the pocket of one of my children. We are very eager to get to the shiny object. But those flashes of inspiration aren't always good for me. I've been known to sacrifice an entire day's agenda on the altar of a new idea.

Can you imagine Paul's years of waiting? Years of idleness sandwiched between a life-changing conversion and a missionary movement. Many theologians believe Paul's three years were spent in prayer, studying Scripture, and careful preparation, and I agree. It makes no sense that following such a transformational encounter with God, he would sit on his hands for three years or return to business as usual. He was a changed man through and through. He would have been filled with excitement and conviction to share his experience and revelation with the masses.

Waiting would have required incredible restraint—rest almost always does.

I have had to practice this type of restraint and intentional waiting with book manuscripts. I can recall many times after a run in the woods, bird-watching walk, or just getting out of the shower when I've eagerly told my husband, "I have a book idea!" Only, with that announcement always comes a somewhat frustrating acknowledgment that an idea is a seed and needs time to germinate.

That was the case with this manuscript. The concept, book proposal, and first week of studies all unfolded from my heart into a computer document within a month. However, the second week wasn't completed until eight months later, not because of procrastination but because the work needed time . . . *I* needed the time.

What work, cause, or purpose do you sense God calling you to that might need time to germinate? What work might God be doing within you to prepare you?

When God reveals something to you by his Word or Spirit, pause. Wait. Rest with it. Follow Jesus into a quiet place and remember Paul's careful preparation. Picture the lodgepole pine cones waiting patiently for the right conditions to fulfill their purpose. God does not rush his work, and we need not either.

### The Roots

> From of old no one has heard
>  or perceived by the ear,
> no eye has seen a God besides you,
>  who acts for those who wait for him.
>  (Isaiah 64:4)

Acts | עָשָׂה | *'āśâ* | aw-saw' | prepare, perform, make, to do

Wait | חָכָה | *ḥākâ* | khaw-kaw' | to wait (in place), to wait (look for), to linger, tarry

### Rest & Reflect

Notice in this Scripture the beautiful harmony between our waiting and God's acting. *Ḥākâ*—to wait—plants our feet in place and directs our eyes forward. It is the epitome of Paul's preparation. He waited in place while eagerly looking forward to what God would do in and through him.

As you *ḥākâ*, planting your feet in faith right where you are, you can look forward with great expectation, resting confidently as God carries out his creative and powerful plan in your life. In what ways do you think God might be calling you to plant your feet in place and wait? What vision, dream, or hope is he drawing you to focus on? Record your thoughts below. Perhaps perform a creative thought and writing exercise by writing out a vivid image of yourself waiting in place and looking toward the horizon to God's plan.

## Under the Microscope

While we gaze toward what God will do, we might also need to glance backward at what he has already accomplished. We find a poignant reminder of this in Psalm 106:13. This verse offers another use of the Hebrew word *ḥāḵâ*, or to wait in place while looking forward. In this instance, it is regarding waiting on God's counsel.

Psalm 106 reflects on God's deliverance of the Israelites from slavery. Verses 1–12 highlight God's steadfast love and sovereign power as he dried up the Red Sea and brought them safely across. Then verse 13 delivers a powerful message: "But they soon forgot his works; they did not wait [*ḥāḵâ*] for his counsel." The Israelites' unwillingness to wait on God's direction was paired with their failure to remember what he'd done in the past.

We can take an important lesson from the Israelites. If you are struggling to wait on God's counsel, look back. Remember how far he's already brought you. Practice remembering with one of these activities:

- Write a prayer of thanks for something significant God did in your life this past year. How did he provide for you? In what ways has he grown your faith?
- Print and hang up photos that represent ways God has blessed you or met you in a need. Consider photos of friends and family, trips, your home, creative projects, and celebrations.
- Every day write down three blessings from God, such as beauty in nature, answered prayers, kind words from a friend, or simple provisions. At the end of each week, read over your lists and thank God for every blessing.
- Ask a trusted friend about how they've seen you grow personally in the last few years.

## WEEK 3

*Day 5*

# BE STILL IN GOD'S
# RESTFUL EMBRACE

SOME ANIMAL BABIES ARE KNOWN for how quickly they become active after birth. Baby horses (foals), for example, can run alongside their mothers within a few hours of birth. Sloths, on the other hand, match the inactivity of their mothers. Immediately after birth, a baby sloth instinctively clings to its mother's fur and will hang on like that for around six months, adopting the mother's pace of life, which is rather slow. Sloths rest for the majority of their time and only move 125 feet or so across the treetops each day. From moving, to eating, to digesting, sloths do everything slowly. And as a sloth baby instinctively clings to its mother during its first half year of life, it can benefit from her unrushed lifestyle. Like a baby sloth sinking into the restful embrace of its mother, we can relax into the restful presence of our heavenly Father. We find an invitation to do exactly that in the words *be still*.

Psalm 46:10 says, "Be still, and know that I am God. I will be exalted among the nations, I will be exalted in the earth!"

We forfeit a lot of powerful truth if we only read a fragment of this verse—"Be still, and know that I am God"—without its surrounding context. Pause a moment and read Psalm 46 in its entirety.

Inside this psalm we hear a declaration of God's power. He is sovereign over natural disasters (vv. 2–3), war, and human authority and powers (vv. 6–9). If he is sovereign over creation, the curse, and humanity, can we not trust him with our circumstances? We can be still knowing "God is our refuge and strength, a very present help in trouble" (v. 1).

"Be still" in Psalm 46:10 is the Hebrew word *rāp̄ â* (רָפָה). It gives the imagery of sinking. And yet God is not telling us to throw our hands up and sink into despair or discouragement. Instead, he is inviting us to sink into his restful embrace. Picture the sloth baby resting in its mother's unhurried pace.

*Rāp̄ â* also means "to release and let go." It reminds me of a swimmer in the ocean struggling to stay above the surface. When a rescue worker arrives, they must convince the swimmer to stop struggling before the worker can bring the swimmer back to safety.

The New American Standard Bible translation captures this well: "Stop striving and know that I am God."

In what ways do you need to let go of control? How do we stop anxiously striving?

"Be still" is our call to stop struggling to make our plans work and sink into God's perfect care and sovereign power. You can practice releasing control using the structure of Psalm 46:10:

1. *Be still.* Stop. Step away from distractions, like technology or noise, and spend a few minutes stilling your heart and mind by focusing on one passage, such as Psalm 23 or Psalm 1:1–3.
2. *Know that I am God.* Focus on what you know is true of God. Write a list beginning with "Know that I am God, who . . ."

We find another example of "be still" in Psalm 37:7: "Be still before the LORD and wait patiently for him; fret not yourself over the one who prospers in his way, over the man who carries out evil devices!" In this verse we find a different Hebrew word often translated as "be still": *dāmam* (דָּמַם). *Dāmam* means "to quiet ourselves and wait." Psalm 37 has a beautiful structure. Open this passage in a physical Bible and look at the paragraph indenting in verses 3–7. Notice the first words in verses 3, 4, 5, and 7. Each one is a verb we are called to do:

- Trust
- Delight
- Commit
- Be still

Practice using this structure to still your racing thoughts or rein in frenzied activity.

- **Trust:** Write down a situation you are choosing to trust God with. When you find yourself trying to control or force your circumstances, surrender your hopes, dreams, and struggles again to God's capable hands.
- **Delight:** Choose a way to delight in God today. Write a note of praise, sing a song, or take a walk in nature.
- **Commit:** Surrender a decision or idea into God's hands. What is something you are struggling to decide on? Ask God for wisdom and guidance and say out loud that you trust his plan no matter the outcome.
- **Be still:** Finally, spend five minutes in silence. Invite God to set your mind and heart at ease.

The next time you hear or read "be still," think about the context of Psalms 46 and 37. Picture yourself letting go of control and sinking into God's restful embrace, and practice quieting your mind and waiting in God's powerful and trustworthy presence.

## The Roots

> He awoke and rebuked the wind and said to the sea, "Peace! Be still!" And the wind ceased, and there was a great calm. (Mark 4:39)

Peace | σιωπάω | *siōpaō* | see-o-pah'-o | to be silent, involuntary stillness, inability to speak

Be still | φιμόω | *phimoō* | fee-mo'-o | to close one's mouth with a muzzle, to be put in check

Calm | γαλήνη | *galēnē* | gal-ay'-nay | tranquility, serenity of the sea

## Rest & Reflect

It is not only in Psalms that we find the words *be still*. Jesus also spoke them from a boat tossing in the raging sea. Jesus speaks the same words into our storms. Sometimes he subdues the circumstances around us. Other times he calms the inner turmoil in our hearts and minds. And in some cases, he might allow situations to persist but provide inner peace and perspective when we seek refuge in his presence. We can cease trying to control outcomes and instead take comfort in Jesus's words "Peace, be still." We can sink into his rest. Consider how he has spoken peace into your life in the past. In what way did he still you? In the words of Oswald Chambers, which we opened our study with, how is God *staying you?*

### Under the Microscope

## MARK 4:37–41

[37] A great windstorm arose, and the waves were breaking into the boat, so that the boat was already filling. [38] But [Jesus] was in the stern, asleep on the cushion. And they woke him and said to him, "Teacher, do you not care that we are perishing?" [39] And he awoke and rebuked the wind and said to the sea, "Peace! Be still!" And the wind ceased, and there was a great calm. [40] He said to them, "Why are you so afraid? Have you still no faith?" [41] And they were filled with great fear and said to one another, "Who then is this, that even the wind and the sea obey him?"

Jesus's use of "Be still!" might seem severe. This was a mandatory stillness. When I asked my Hebrew and Greek editor about the word Jesus used for "be still," he said it has modern connotations of "Be quiet already" or "Silence!"

Jesus brought creation into submission with his breath and reminded the sea of its place under his sovereignty. Psalm 95:5 says, "The sea is his, for he made it." Through Christ, all things were made (John 1:3), and here we see him using the power of his word, which created the sea, to turn its tossing waters into a serene and smooth surface.

I wonder, at times, if he takes the same approach with us. "Be still" can be a gentle invitation, or it can be a loving yet harsh correction. Perhaps if, for too long, we neglect his invitation to be still, he voices it a little more forcefully.

# WEEK 3

*Days 6 and 7*

# STOP & DELIGHT

## COME AWAY AND REST

FIND AN *ERĒMOS* (QUIET PLACE) and make it your own. It can be a natural area in your town or a route along a pond, lake, or river. It might be in your own yard or in a public garden or park. Plan to visit this place a few times in the coming weeks and associate the location with prayer. Let it be where you accept Jesus's invitation to "Come with me by yourselves to a quiet place and get some rest" (Mark 6:31 NIV).

The first time you visit, take note of the sounds, colors, and categories of nature. Are there birds, bugs, snow, bushes, berries, trees? What kind of trees? What shape are the leaves? What does the birdsong sound like? Practice noticing the details of God's designs while sitting with him in a quiet place.

### Journaling Questions

Where have you felt at rest? Describe the surroundings. Were you inside or outside? What was the scenery? Was a candle lit? Was music playing? What was the temperature?

Is there a dream or idea you sense God calling you to? Practice a prayerful pause and ask God to bring perspective for moving forward in his good timing.

What is your reaction to the words *be still*? Do they feel trite or overused? Unrealistic? Comforting? How has your perspective of God's invitation to be still changed this week?

# WEEK 4

## SELAH
## Experiencing Daily Rest

*The steadfast love of the LORD never ceases;*
*his mercies never come to an end;*
*they are new every morning;*
*great is your faithfulness.*

LAMENTATIONS 3:22–23

# WEEK 4

*Day 1*

# REST NOTES

IN MUSICAL COMPOSITION, REST NOTES indicate pauses or intervals of silence between musical notes. Birds have something similar to rest notes in their song compositions. Between syllables or phrases, a bird will take minibreaths, which are short, thirty-millisecond breaths unperceived except by dramatically slowing down a recorded birdsong. They are more functional than poetic, allowing a bird enough air to carry its song for impressive durations.

The psalmists penned similar rest notes into their work using the word *selah*.

*Selah* is a puzzling word for Bible readers and scholars alike. Although the original meaning is uncertain, it's believed to lend musical, liturgical, or literary direction. It acts as an intentional stop or redirection. It is a cue to pause.

Like the birds practicing minibreaths to carry their melodies, psalmists intentionally used the word *selah* to signify a pause between thoughts. Songs, the psalms, and creation remind us that catching our breath is necessary for carrying on well in our work.

The irony of the word *selah* is that, due to its puzzling nature and pronunciation (SUH-lah, SEE-lah, or SAY-lah), we are apt to skip right over it, as if it's a footnote.

Because it's cloaked in mystery, we might think selah is only relevant to its original culture and audience. Yet consider selah in light of 2 Timothy 3:16–18: "All Scripture is breathed out by God and profitable for teaching, for reproof, for correction, and for training in righteousness, that the man of God may be complete, equipped for every good work." Every word of Scripture is intentional, including *selah*. And if selah is a signal to pause, then pausing is helpful for teaching, reproof, correction, and training in righteousness.

Selah is meant to be much more than a footnote; it is instead a highlight. It is our signal to stop and reflect and to wait for God's nudge before continuing.

We are notorious for skipping over moments of pause in our lives. We jump from one activity to the next, similar to the way we might skim over the word *selah* in Psalms. But I'm afraid that when we fail to pause as we transition, we hurriedly pass right by opportunities for God to transform us. We forfeit times of celebration, lament, thanksgiving, repentance, or whatever God has for us between this moment and the next.

Let's break that habit this week because selah might be more relevant now than ever before.

At the outset of this week, let me assure you that a selah pause is not a practice of taking catnaps throughout the day (although it may include that). More than napping, selah pauses often take the form of intentional relaxing or an energizing and inspiring activity, such as a walk in the sunshine, a cup of tea, a chapter of a book, a conversation with a friend, or a view of the sunrise. They are the moments between activities, to give us the space needed to fuel our effectiveness in God's kingdom. What I have often found is that during these selah pauses, God lends us perspective. Poking our heads up from preoccupations, we might realize that what we are busy with isn't a vital activity, that perhaps it's out of line with our values or what is most important. Selah pauses provide the space for God to redirect our attention and align our activities with his agenda.

What demands your attention the most in this season? It might be a very real and worthwhile need, such as a newborn baby, ailing parent, or exciting career or ministry. However, even worthwhile responsibilities that we consider vital activities need pauses in order to thrive. How might you build in moments of selah into your current responsibilities?

**The Roots**

> I cried aloud to the LORD,
> and he answered me from his holy hill. *Selah*
> (Psalm 3:4)

Cried | קָרָא | *qārā'* | kaw-raw' | to call unto, proclaim

Answered | עָנָה | *'ānâ* | aw-naw' | respond, make a reply

Selah | סֶלָה | *selê* | se'-leh | to lift up and exalt, suspension (of music), pause

**Rest & Reflect**

It is worth noticing that King David paused after an interaction with God. He called out and invited God's presence and input. God responded, and then David sat with God's reply in a selah pause. When we cry to God, we must pause long enough to allow him to lean in and provide direction or comfort. When we receive insight from his Word or Spirit, that truth can root down deeper as we process it by journaling, praying, or walking in nature as we soak in his answer. What insights are being revealed to you today? What's the best way for you to pause and process God's truth in your life?

### Under the Microscope

Psalm 3:2 is the first mention of the word *selah* in the Scriptures, and we see it three times in the chapter. It is a beautiful example of selah as a call to pause, rest, reflect, then redirect. Read Psalm 3 below and consider King David's thoughts. He seems to preach to himself as he progresses through a revelation and remembrance of God's faithfulness.

As you read, circle every mention of *selah* and write "pause" next to it.

## PSALM 3

¹ O LORD, how many are my foes!
    Many are rising against me;
² many are saying of my soul,
    "There is no salvation for him in God." *Selah*

³ But you, O LORD, are a shield about me,
    my glory, and the lifter of my head.

<sup>4</sup> I cried aloud to the LORD,
  and he answered me from his holy hill. *Selah*

<sup>5</sup> I lay down and slept;
  I woke again, for the LORD sustained me.
<sup>6</sup> I will not be afraid of many thousands of people
  who have set themselves against me all around.

<sup>7</sup> Arise, O LORD!
  Save me, O my God!
For you strike all my enemies on the cheek;
  you break the teeth of the wicked.

<sup>8</sup> Salvation belongs to the LORD;
  your blessing be on your people! *Selah*

- What is King David's focus in verses 1–2?
- What is his focus in verses 3–4, and how does the focus shift from verses 1–2? Pay attention to the pivotal word *but* in verse 3.
- What is the focus in verses 5–8? What perspective does David end the psalm with?

# WEEK 4

*Day 2*

# CIRCADIAN REST

CIRCADIAN COMES FROM TWO LATIN words: *Circa*, meaning "around," and *diem*, meaning "day." *Circadian* translates to "around a day." In science, *circadian rhythm* refers to how a twenty-four-hour period affects us mentally, physically, and behaviorally. Our bodies innately react to the position of the sun in the sky, taking cues from sunrise, sunset, and the sun's relation to us in between those times. I would argue that circadian rhythm also affects us spiritually.

We see circadian rhythm initiated during creation, when God created lights to guide time, as we read in Genesis 1:16: "God made the two great lights—the greater light to rule the day and the lesser light to rule the night—and the stars."

Humankind harnessed illumination through the invention of electric lighting, and while these advancements have brought many benefits to society, one drawback is that it widened the circle for "around a day." With the introduction of the light bulb, humans have gone from an average of ten hours of sleep a night to seven.[1] We have stretched a day like an expanding balloon being inflated beyond its limits. It's bound to pop.

God designed our bodies to thrive on a regular sleep schedule, which collaborates with our bodies' natural processes. I have often joked that sleep is my superpower. (Those who are insomniacs, please don't hate me right now.) Because of Addison's disease and a lack of the cortisol hormone, my body doesn't have a natural wake trigger. While many people with too high of cortisol levels are kept up at night, I am in deep sleep within three minutes of lying down and sleep hard through the night. However, my superpower is also one of my most significant challenges. Without a natural cortisol peak in the morning, my body doesn't wake up like most. Many days one of the hardest things I do is get out of bed, which is problematic for my work. I need to wake well before sunrise to spend time in silence, solitude, and prayer and to accomplish all I set out to do.

Author Bruce Barton wrote, "Jesus was an early riser; he knew that the simplest way to live *more* than an average life is to add an hour to the fresh end of the day."[2]

I want to be like Jesus. But some mornings, the pillow calls louder than the Spirit.

My health condition is uncommon, but many people suffer from the opposite condition of elevated cortisol levels due to stress. And that too can wreak havoc on our sleep patterns. Both too little or too much cortisol represent the curse of sin and the disruption to God's pattern of rest.

Cortisol is a critical player in our circadian rhythm, often called our internal clock. God engineered our bodies to operate in beautiful synchrony with our exterior environment. One study said, "The circadian system coordinates physiology and behaviors towards the environment in such a way that the body acts like a finely harmonized clock."[3]

God carefully tuned our internal clocks to work in tandem with nature's circadian cues, namely the rising and setting of the sun.

However, when creation was broken by sin, so were our circadian rhythms and natural cycles of rest. Whether or not your body appropriately doles out the cortisol hormone, you likely face physical, mental, and even spiritual challenges in experiencing God's gift of daily circadian rest.

If you struggle with sleep, you've likely already researched methods to help, such as listening to calm music, drinking chamomile tea, turning off screens an hour before bed, or spraying calming scents on your pillow. I want to suggest a different approach I've taken over the past few years.

A powerful way to tune our internal, God-given clocks is by noticing circadian rhythms in nature. God tuned nature with dependable rhythms, or a standard of time we can defer to. Nature's sunrise-sunset clock is an authoritative reference for God's perfect pattern of rest and work. Day is for work and night is for rest. Of course you might work the night shift at the hospital or the swing shift on the factory floor, but the principle remains. There is a time for sleep and a time for work. When we let work overflow into sleep or vice versa, we've upset the balance God created us to have.

Although creation is broken, we can still glimpse God's original design and allow it to inform our patterns of work and rest. One way I've done this is to become a collector of sunrises and sunsets. You can do the same by letting the sun's rising and setting be your cue to pause. Let these stunning moments when God paints the sky with color be your selah signal to be still for a few minutes. Pause and admire God's design of time reflected in nature. Go for a walk at sunrise and notice which birds take up the first morning songs. Which species are the early risers? Or walk through your neighborhood at dusk and notice how nature seems to hush as the sun falls below the horizon.

This week commit yourself to collecting a few sunrises and sunsets and using creation to tune your internal clock.

## The Roots

> The steadfast love of the LORD never ceases;
> his mercies never come to an end;
> they are new every morning;
> great is your faithfulness.
>
> (Lamentations 3:22–23)

Steadfast love | חֶסֶד | *ḥeseḏ* | kheh'-sed | goodness, kindness, mercy, loyalty

Mercies | רַחַם | *raḥam* | rakh'-am | compassion, deep feeling of parental love

New | חָדָשׁ | *ḥāḏāš* | khaw-dawsh' | fresh

Faithfulness | אֱמוּנָה | *ĕmûnâ* | em-oo-naw' | fidelity, steadiness, stability

## Rest & Reflect

The richness and depth of this passage can easily be lost on us if we read words like *steadfast love, mercies,* and *faithfulness* through a lens of familiarity. They can become muddied together, losing their unique qualities. As we extract the original meaning from the Hebrew words, we discover the breadth of God's devotion to us. His affection and loyalty spread like a root system, holding up our lives and nourishing our souls. Every day God causes the sun to rise and set.

God is both stable and steady. His fidelity or loyalty to us is unmatched. He loves us as a perfect Father, true to his unchanging nature of goodness and kindness. Every dawn we can rise to the richness of his love, new and fresh for the day ahead. Consider how your God-given circadian rhythm might be off balance. Where are you allowing work to bleed into rest time? Write a prayer below asking God to restore rhythms of rest as you take notice of his patterns in nature.

### Under the Microscope

Psalm 92 is titled "A Song for the Sabbath," and I love how it alludes to circadian rhythm. Read verses 1–2:

> ¹ It is good to give thanks to the LORD,
>     to sing praises to your name, O Most High;
> ² to declare your steadfast love in the morning,
>     and your faithfulness by night.

King David was onto something here. Maybe he was in tune with human nature and how morning is often a time most conducive to praise. We hear the birds singing and feel the warmth of the returning sun, and we give thanks for God's steadfast love reflected in new morning mercies.

Evening, however, holds the weight of a day. Maybe there were challenges, setbacks, and grievances. It is harder to praise God from fatigue and overwhelm, and yet perhaps that is when our praise is most mature. This is when our focus changes from God's steadfast love to his faithfulness. In the night, in the dark, we recall what he did in the light and remember that the sun will rise again tomorrow. This is a circadian rhythm of praise.

This week, practice worshiping God in the morning, perhaps with the sunrise, through prayer, singing, or journaling praise to him as you consider his steadfast love. A time of morning worship and prayer is often called *matin*. It creates space for delighting in the new day God has brought forth and acknowledging him at the outset of our activities. In literary terms, *matin* can refer to the morning melody of birds, which birdwatchers refer to as the *dawn chorus*. Join in the dawn chorus with a time of matin prayer and worship. Sing praise to God, interluded with times of silence and prayer. Focus on delight and thanksgiving more than requests. What characteristic of God are you grateful for today? His unconditional love? Unmatched power? Unending grace? What blessings can you thank him for before any needs of the day press in?

In the evening, with the sunset, reflect on the day and write down ways God was faithful. A time of prayer and reflection at the day's end is often referred to as *examen*. Examen is different from matin. Examen, as it sounds, is a time of examining or reflecting back on the experiences of your day. What challenges did you encounter? Is God already showing up in those difficulties, or can you pray for clarity and help? Examen is a time to pinpoint where you saw God's activities and providence throughout the day.

*Circadian Rest*

# WEEK 4

## Day 3

# NATURE'S CLOCK

THROUGHOUT HISTORY, HUMANKIND HAS SOUGHT to harness time and fragment it into increasingly small measurements. Units of time began large and with nature. God created light and separated it from darkness, initiating the first day. Genesis 1:14 tells us God then hung lights in the sky to guide seasons, days, and years.

In the Old Testament, the Hebrew word יוֹם or *yôm* (pronounced yome) is translated as "day." Two ways Scripture uses the word is to (1) communicate the time of daylight between dawn to dusk, and (2) indicate the sun returning to the same spot in the sky. In the New Testament, we find the new and smaller time unit of an hour, conveyed in the Greek word ὥρα or *hŏra* (pronounced ho'-rah). *Hŏra* can refer to one-twelfth the time of daylight in a day (which changes throughout the year), or an imprecise division of a day. It can also be used to communicate something immediate. Where we might say "at this moment," New Testament language might say "at this hour." An imprecise hour (*hŏra*) is the smallest measurement of time used in Scripture. And so in the Bible, time is governed, tracked, and understood in light of (no pun intended) nature, and is only ever as small as an imprecise hour.

However, as society developed, needs arose for finer time measurements. Mankind learned to divide a day into more precise measurements using sun and star positions. Sundials were developed to track daylight hours, and the Babylonians divided an hour into sixty minutes and a minute into sixty seconds.

Even in the second century BC, some in society sensed the stifling nature of measuring time. Aquilius wrote a Roman comedy including a character who complained against the popular new technology of sundials and the rigid controls they placed on his days. He lamented, "May the gods destroy that man who first discovered hours, the very man who first set up a sundial here, who smashed my day, alas, into fragments."[1]

What would Aquilius and his contemporaries think of our further fragmentation of time? The smallest unit of time scientists have measured is a zeptosecond, which is a trillionth of a billionth of a second. Written out, it is 0.000000000000000000001 of a second.

Humankind has an obsession with tracking time. Perhaps it gives us a notion of control or ownership. Certainly, an awareness of time helps us be faithful. Psalm 90:12 instructs us to "number our days that we may get a heart of wisdom." Scripture's regular reminders of how short our lives are give us a healthy sense of urgency and spur us on to good works that ripple into eternity. And yet for most of us, time is not an ally but a constant tension. There never seems to be enough of it. Our preoccupation with measuring time and ordering our lives down to the nanosecond can leave us with a scarcity mindset.

We often only think of time in a linear, chronological manner. And it makes sense, to some degree, that we pay attention to linear, chronological time. After all, there are times when my kids do need to have their shoes on and be in the car in twenty minutes in order for us to get to jujitsu class in time. And if they want time to stop at the library on the way home, I need to get dinner in the pressure cooker now so we don't have to cook later. Chronological time is always top of mind. It guides us through our time-stamped days. Yet it can also make us rushed and restless.

Time is meant to hold much more than zeptoseconds; time contains the moments that make up our lives. Time is both two dimensional (chronological) and three dimensional (deep and full of meaning). Consider this example from my life:

- My first son was born at 9:19 p.m. on July 18, 2011 (chronological).
- Everything changed the moment my son was born. I became a mother for the first time (deep).

Both statements speak about the same moment, but the second extracts the meaning and purpose from that minute on the clock. A child's birth is a powerful example, but consider your everyday life. If we are too focused on linear, chronological time, we miss the depth of moments that make up our lives. Time remains shallow.

I experienced deep time in a profound way in my teenage years when I traveled to tribal communities in Africa and Southeast Asia. I particularly remember church services in Malawi, Africa. I was fourteen and had grown up in church. I was used to carefully planned service times with a half hour between for cookies (my mom baked hundreds of them each Sunday), juice, and fellowship in the gym. When it was time for the second service, my dad rang the large church bell from the sanctuary tower, and we kids knew it was time to get off the playground and join the adults for service.

Malawi was different. I don't know if anyone really knew what time service began. Eventually, rhythmic, energetic worship enlivened the wood, brick, and mud sanctuary. Pews filled, and service began for who knows how long, because no one really knew when it ended either. We were there to be together in the Word, Spirit, and worship. Chronological time had little bearing on the people of Malawi. The focus on depth and nature's rhythms left wide-open spaces for meaningful moments and both vital work and vital rest.

How might we return to a more nature-paced lifestyle? How can we operate by nature's clock rather than tightly pack our schedules down to the zeptosecond?

One way is to return to larger units for measuring time. When we fragment time down to tiny units, it can give a false sense of having more time to fill. If, instead, we view our days in larger segments, we are less likely to overpack them. Consider returning to the Romans' practice before sundials were common, when they divided a day into large segments, including sunrise to the beginning of the third hour, forenoon, afternoon, and the ninth or tenth hour until sunset. All of this was governed by the sun's passage through the sky.

Of course we can't tell a friend we'll meet them at the coffee shop "at the beginning of the third hour after sunrise." However, we can practice a realistic and honest approach to scheduling our days in larger chunks, with more margin around each activity or event, allowing time for selah pauses and to notice the sun's position above as it guides the passing hours. Consider time blocking, or dividing the time on your calendar, by hours. If an activity only fills one half of an hour, refrain from filling the other half. Don't allow two commitments to immediately butt up against each other. Instead, practice creating pockets of empty time in the form of fifteen to thirty minutes. More often than not, activities and responsibilities take more time than we allot to them, leaving us stressed and behind schedule. Create uncommitted spaces in your agenda and use those opportunities to practice selah pauses, taking time to regroup, pray, and gain perspective.

### The Roots

> As for man, his days are like grass;
> he flourishes like a flower of the field.
> (Psalm 103:15)

Grass | חָצִיר | *ḥāṣîr* | khaw-tseer' | grass, herbage, reed, quickly perishing

Flower | צִיץ | *ṣîṣ* | tseets | bloom, blossom, shining

Flourishes | צוּץ | *ṣûṣ* | tsoots | blossom, shine, gleam

### Rest & Reflect

Notice in this verse how our days (chronological time) are likened to grass. Yet we ourselves are compared to a flower. A flower, like grass, is fleeting. It quickly perishes. Scripture is clear that our time on earth is short. And yet in that limited reality, we are meant to flourish and bloom. Consider the perennial flowers we learned about in week 1, which come back stronger and more brilliant each year as their roots strengthen. We cannot change the amount of chronological time we are given—only God knows the number of our days. He wants us to use our time on vital activities that align with our values and his agenda and to experience deep, profound moments that breathe life into chronological time and make it so much more than the passing of days. Write down an idea or two for adjusting how you plan your days. How can you add margin between activities and avoid packing things in too tightly?

## Under the Microscope

Psalm 90 is Moses's beautiful prayer, in which he lines up God's everlasting nature with humankind's fleeting time on earth. Verses 1–11 depict chronological time. Notice these key observations:

- "From everlasting to everlasting you are God" (v. 2). (Although *everlasting* refers to eternity, it's still used in this context as a measurement of time.)
- "You return man to dust" (v. 3).
- "For a thousand years in your sight are but as yesterday when it is past" (v. 4).
- "The years of our life are seventy, or even by reason of strength eighty; yet their span is but toil and trouble; they are soon gone, and we fly away" (v. 10).

Write down seasons of your life when it felt time was flying by. When have you been caught up by the passing of days? Maybe it was while raising children, building a career, or immersed in ministry. Those times are meaningful and can certainly be a part of our vital work. As we transition to Moses's focus on deep time, see if you can pull out deep and meaningful moments in those busy seasons.

Verse 12 pivots to the deep meaning of time as Moses switches from observation to practical takeaways and requests:

- "So teach us to number our days that we may get a heart of wisdom" (v. 12). Since our time on earth is short, we can ask God to help us to measure and manage our lives as God originally intended—keeping an eye on both vital work and vital rest.
- "Satisfy us in the morning with your steadfast love, that we may rejoice and be glad all our days" (v. 14). Let us enjoy our short time as we live in God's love and delight.

Consider the unique passions and interests God created you with. Do you enjoy art? Music? Nature? Reading? Take time to delight in what God created you to enjoy.

- "Establish the work of our hands upon us; yes, establish the work of our hands!" (v. 17). Let our work be purposeful and performed with trust in and reliance on God's power.

Write down some profound moments you have experienced in life. It might be the birth of a child, a meaningful conversation, a wedding day, or an experience with God. Look back through photos if you need inspiration. Pinpoint where you have experienced deep time. Consider how you can make more space for those moments moving forward.

As we live in linear time (Psalm 90:1–11), we can experience our vital purpose by trusting that God not only *knows* what is best for us but also *wants* what is best for us and his kingdom (vv. 12–17). Ultimately God wants us to find the joy and purpose in following his plan.

# WEEK 4

### Day 4

# SETTING A RESTFUL PACE

IN THE WILD, ANIMALS FILL their days with vital activities. They are focused on survival and reproduction, reflecting their God-given initiative to produce after their own kind. They hunt, gather, reproduce, and seek shelter. My family and I see this every autumn when we go up to watch the elk in rut season in Rocky Mountain National Park. It is fascinating and exhausting to watch. The male bull elk are busy gathering female cows and calves into small groups, called *harems*, and protecting them from rival males. The elk are solely focused on reproducing, finding food and shelter, and staying safe. These are their vital activities.

Although our vital activities look different from the animal kingdom's, we can learn from nature about prioritizing what matters. When we wake, what is the first thing we think or do? Are we neglecting any of our values like faith, marriage, parenting, personal growth, community, or health?

Discontent and unrest rise when there is a tension between our values and lifestyle. When I value spending time with my family but I'm not making space in our calendar for walks outside together or board games around the table, my soul is not at rest. I often feel this tension when I neglect to set a restful pace in life.

As I practice writing margin into our calendar, saying no to most commitments or activities and giving my time to what I value most, a deep and settling peace returns. Setting a restful pace frees us from frantic and reactive living so we can live intentionally and spend our time on what is truly vital to our minds, bodies, souls, and families. It is time to get greedy about our time in the best of ways, take back what God has given us, and employ it for good and growth.

It's up to you and me to make the most important things . . . the most important things. Think about a bear preparing for winter. Although they don't truly hibernate, bears go through a time of hyperphagia before cold weather sets in. This is when a bear eats around twenty thousand calories a day to increase its body weight by 20 to 30 percent. During this time of preparing for winter, if a bear woke and was immediately distracted, giving its time to frivolous things, it would sacrifice crucial time for vital activities like foraging and bulking up fat stores.

Many of us have heard the illustration of a jar, rocks, and sand. The jar represents our time, the rocks represent our values, and the sand is everything else. The only way to get the big meaningful things (rocks) into the jar is to put them in first, and then add the smaller things (sand) to fit around the rocks. If we fill the jar with sand first, there is no room left for rocks. I have one of these jars on my shelf as a reminder to fill my time with what is most important first. When I filled the jar, what struck me was that I had leftover sand. Had I begun filling the jar with sand (minor things) instead of rocks (values), the jar would have fit every grain of sand. But because I began with rocks, representing things like faith, family, rest, purposeful work, and health, there wasn't enough room left for all the sand grains. The point is this: By filling our time first with what we value, the excess is edited out.

This is how I set a pace as I begin each day: I front-load the day with what matters most. I walk the neighborhood just after dawn to listen to the birds. I work out before the passing of hours, which wear on my motivation. I enjoy coffee with my husband as we discuss the day before us. I sit and read my kids a book before I start a work project. I don't do each of these things every day. However, as I practice intentionally placing them at the front end of my days, they happen more often. Think about the rocks and sand, which relate back to God's pattern at creation: Rest comes first. If we fill our time with everything else, we won't have time for the vital activity of rest. Our day's vital work depends on us beginning with rest.

By identifying and front-loading what's most important, you'll combat the temptation to rush through your day, hoping you'll eventually get to what matters . . . if there is leftover time. Don't risk running out of hours before getting to what matters most.

We can set a restful pace not only for our days but also for months and years. Approaching a new month feels fresh and full of potential. My kids are always eager for their turn to flip the paper calendar on the first day of a new month. I then sit down with it and write whatever is on the digital calendar I use to plan our year. This way we're all on the same page about how the month unfolds.

However, as I transfer events and commitments from the digital calendar and the white space on the paper calendar fills, I'm always surprised by how much we've said yes to in advance.

I have learned that I need to practice restraint months ahead. Suppose it is January, and friends ask us to come to dinner in March. In that case, I add it to our March calendar, noting we are officially planning two months out. I must carefully protect time in March, or we'll arrive at March 1 and already have no margin.

By keeping a digital calendar that all other calendars refer to, you can block out times and even entire days that are untouchable. You can dramatically dial back the pace of your life by building in margin months in advance. It's simple—if we make no margin, there will be no margin.

By choosing ahead of time what you will and will not allow into a day, month, and year, you can practice control of the pace of your life and ensure there is ample time for vital activities, including rest. Wherever you are at in the calendar month, look at the four weeks ahead of you. Consider each commitment made and which values it reflects. Are each of your commitments or responsibilities vital activities supporting what matters most? Consider which ones are extra fluff or not contributing much (or anything) to your most important values. Decide now how you can respectfully back out of those opportunities or phase out of them in the coming months.

### The Roots

> Look carefully then how you walk, not as unwise but as wise, making the best use of the time, because the days are evil. Therefore do not be foolish, but understand what the will of the Lord is. (Ephesians 5:15–17)

Carefully | ἀκριβῶς | *akribōs* | ak-ree-boce' | exactly, accurately, diligently

Wise | σοφός | *sophos* | sof-os' | skilled, to act wisely, experienced, clever, learned

### Rest & Reflect

Setting a healthy, restful pace is a powerful way we can make "the best use of the time." As we align our pace with God's and fall into step with him, we can better understand his will for our lives. Notice the author's use of the word *carefully*. Especially considering today's connected world with abounding opportunities, requests, and demands on your time, what can you cut out to be diligent—ruthless, even—in protecting your time for vital activities?

## Under the Microscope

"Ah, stubborn children" is not a great way to be greeted. But this is how God addressed the Israelites in Isaiah 30. God had a good reason for calling out his people. He said they were a people "who carry out a plan, but not mine." God continued by pointing out where they went wrong, including seeking refuge in fallible humans without his direction, which he said would become their shame and humiliation.

Have you ever attempted to carry out a plan that wasn't God's? Maybe it was a big plan regarding a relationship, move, or career. Or our prideful "I've got this" moment might be in an area that doesn't seem like a big deal. We might rush into accepting an opportunity because it is exciting, without first weighing the cost of time and energy. We can easily fall into the trap of stubbornness in our day-to-day lives. As you and I go through a day, are we attempting to carry out a plan that God does not have his hand in? Are we setting a pace he doesn't want for us?

In Isaiah 30:13 God gives a powerful visual to show the result of the Israelite's wandering: "Therefore this iniquity shall be to you like a breach in a high wall, bulging out and about to collapse, whose breaking comes suddenly, in an instant."

When we intentionally turn away from God's plan or pace, we

are bound to break. Pursuing our plans without God's hand leads to restless, fast-paced, unsustainable living. Is your life's wall breached? Has following your personal agenda away from God's direction left you vulnerable? Choose this moment to repent. Lay your plans at the feet of Jesus.

Pray this prayer: *Lord, I surrender my desires and what I think is best. Your best is better. Help me carry out your work for me at your pace, in your power, and for your glory. Amen.*

The good news is that God didn't leave the Israelites helpless, and he doesn't abandon us either.

Despite the Israelites' wandering, God offered them hope. Follow these steps as you read verses from Isaiah 30 below.

- Circle *returning and rest* and write an idea or two that can help you return to and rest in God's plan and pace.
- Circle *quietness and in trust* and write one or two things you are choosing to trust God with so you can rest in his pace and provision.

## ISAIAH 30:15, 18, 20–21

<sup>15</sup> For thus said the Lord GOD, the Holy One of Israel,
  "In returning and rest you shall be saved;
    in quietness and in trust shall be your strength." . . .

<sup>18</sup> Therefore the LORD waits to be gracious to you,
    and therefore he exalts himself to show mercy to you.
  For the LORD is a God of justice;
    blessed are all those who wait for him.

. . . <sup>20</sup> And though the Lord give you the bread of adversity
  and the water of affliction, yet your Teacher will not hide

himself anymore, but your eyes shall see your Teacher. [21] And your ears shall hear a word behind you, saying, "This is the way, walk in it," when you turn to the right or when you turn to the left.

When we trade our agendas and paces for God's, we can rest in his strength, grace, and direction. How can you return to his rest this week? Is there an opportunity you rushed into and are now regretting or second-guessing? Ask him to grant clarity and to quiet your spirit as you trust his guidance and provision.

# WEEK 4

## Day 5

# RESTING FROM
# INFORMATION OVERLOAD

WHEN GOD DESIGNED BIRDS, HE was simultaneously filling the sky with examples of daily rest, or regular selah pauses. We have already seen how hummingbirds sustain their activity through torpor and how songbirds insert minibreaths into their melodies. Now let's look at another bird that models a rhythm of regular rest: the great frigate bird.

The great frigate bird is unique to the seabird world in that it cannot swim. Partly because of their lack of landing spots, a frigate bird remains in the sky for up to two months without touching any surface or landing. A frigate bird stays aloft through a strategy called *unihemispheric sleep*, where one half of its brain turns off, allowing the creature to sleep, while the other half remains alert to any dangers and, in the case of the frigate bird, allows it to fly on a God-engineered autopilot system.

The great frigate is a powerful example of filtering the amount of information entering our brains. How much of our anxiety and unrest is the result of information overload? Like the great frigate, we can practice being aware of peripheral danger while remaining at rest and focused on vital activities. We will have a difficult time practicing regular selah rest in our days if our minds are constantly running with anxious thoughts. By being selective about what we fill our minds with, we can more easily enjoy rest on a daily basis.

We are not meant to be unaware of what's going on in the world. On the contrary, in Micah 6:8 God calls us "to do justice, and to love kindness, and to walk humbly with [our] God." We are to love God and others and to care for widows, orphans, and those in hard circumstances. We cannot do those things without being aware of the needs around us and abroad. However, being *too* aware is a threat to our peace and rest. We are simply not meant to know every tragedy and tension happening across the globe. Only God has the brainpower and emotional capacity to hold the world's burdens.

One way I filter information is by not scouring news websites or following news feeds. Instead, I trust a few good friends to tell me what they know might affect me concerning world events. Further, with our kids I watch *WORLD Watch*, a news resource with a biblical worldview that shares critical events and information and, importantly, how we can pray for needs around the world. My children and I watch this daily program then, from the content, create a short list of prayer requests and pray together for needs around the world. You can intentionally choose one or two news sources you trust and unfollow and avoid other sources that bring only anxiety.

What other flows of unnecessary information can you cut off?

To help you consider how much and what kind of information you take in on an average day, make a list of specific sources of information that you consider vital. Maybe they are books, apps, social media accounts, or communication with specific people. Then go through the list looking for outlets that

- point your attention to Jesus;
- are life-giving to your mind and spirit;

- inspire and encourage you;
- make you laugh and are wholesome;
- keep you connected to loved ones; or
- keep you informed on critical things. (And be super ruthless when deciding what you truly need to know and cutting out the rest.)

Now go through the list and mark information sources that make you unrestful, maybe things that

- leave you feeling anxious;
- go against God's Word;
- are completely unrelated to you;
- leave you feeling like you wasted time;
- distract you from vital things, like spending time in God's Word, with family, or on your mental or physical health; or
- make you feel like you need to do more or be more to keep up with others.

Filtering out unnecessary information may include unfollowing accounts, unsubscribing to email lists, and uninstalling apps.

We cannot be a champion for every cause or volunteer for every nonprofit meeting needs around the world, but we can carefully choose a few needs to pray diligently for and, if God leads, get involved in. We're also not meant to process the vast amounts of information flowing through our social media feeds each day. Instead, we can intentionally choose to consume content that encourages us and nurtures our God-given gifts and interests, while unfollowing and filtering out things that leave us anxious or distracted.

We can be like the great frigate bird, taking a measured and strategic risk on rest and filtering out unnecessary distractions so we can continue well and safely on our way.

*The Roots*

> You keep him in perfect peace
> whose mind is stayed on you,
> because he trusts in you.
>
> (Isaiah 26:3)

Stayed | סָמַךְ | *sāmak* | saw-mak' | rested, upheld, sustained

Trusts | בָּטַח | *bāṭaḥ* | baw-takh' | confidence, security, to feel safe

*Rest & Reflect*

Our complex and creative minds naturally flow from one thought, theme, and concept to another. It's easy for our minds to wander. Yet as we practice keeping our minds fixed on Jesus, perfect peace becomes, as it was meant to be, our natural state. Notice the word for *stayed* can mean "rested." Practice resting your thoughts on God. Tell him what you want to filter out so you can more readily and consistently focus on the vital activities that he has for you to do.

*Under the Microscope*

God's Word heavily emphasizes the importance of protecting our minds. God created our brains to be incredibly complex and sophisticated. In a world cursed by sin, that means our very capable brains are vulnerable to distraction and anxious thoughts. Second Corinthians 10:5 instructs us to "take every thought captive to obey Christ." As we saw today, we can begin to take every thought captive by filtering out harmful, unhelpful, or distracting inputs. Read Ephesians 4:11–16 below.

- Circle *knowledge of the Son of God* in verse 13 and *speaking the truth* in verse 15. Draw a line connecting those concepts.
- Put a star by *knowledge of the Son of God*. Refer to the first list you wrote today. Next to the star, copy down your list of sources that point you to God. If you run out of room in the margin, use the journaling space below.
- Underline *waves, wind of doctrine, human cunning, craftiness,* and *deceitful schemes.*

## EPHESIANS 4:11-16

[11] And he gave the apostles, the prophets, the evangelists, the shepherds and teachers, [12] to equip the saints for the work of ministry, for building up the body of Christ, [13] until we all attain to the unity of the faith and of the knowledge of the Son of God, to mature manhood, to the measure of the stature of the fullness of Christ, [14] so that we may no longer be children, tossed to and fro by the waves and carried about by every wind of doctrine, by human cunning, by craftiness in deceitful schemes. [15] Rather, speaking the truth in love, we are to grow up in every way into him who is the head, into Christ, [16] from whom the whole body, joined and held together by every joint with which it is equipped, when each part is working properly, makes the body grow so that it builds itself up in love.

What sources of information deliver harmful information? Write those here and ask God to help you cut those influences off at their source.

# WEEK 4

*Days 6 and 7*

# STOP & DELIGHT

## PRACTICE SELAH PAUSES

OVER THE NEXT WEEK, SET a timer to go off several times each day, perhaps even every hour. Let it be your cue to practice a selah pause. Remember, *selah* can mean to "pause," "rest," "meditate on," "redirect." Stop for several minutes to stand, go for a walk, pour a cup of tea, listen to a worship song, pray, or give thanks. You don't need to commit to this for the long haul. Instead, try it for a couple of days and see what happens. Invite God to speak to you in those moments and to fuel you for the next hour. Consider writing down your experience or a few words he gives you as you pause.

### Journaling Questions

Do you have a memory of watching a particular sunrise or sunset? Take time to write about that memory. Or if you don't have one, create one this week by viewing a sunrise or sunset. Record your thoughts and reactions as you practice paying attention and stepping into creation's circadian rhythms.

What areas of your day feel rushed? Picture a map app that shows an upcoming traffic jam as red on your route. Identify those red zones in your days. Where is the tension of hurry? Consider how you can create margin between activities, and practice saying no in order to operate at a restful pace.

How are you experiencing information overload? Commit to filter out unnecessary information inputs and become selective in what you allow into your mind over the next few days so you can remain restful throughout your day.

# WEEK 5

## SABBATH
## Practicing Weekly Rest

*So then, there remains a Sabbath rest for the
people of God.*

HEBREWS 4:9

# WEEK 5

## *Day 1*

# A WEEKLY RHYTHM
# OF REST

NATURE DOES NOT NEED PERMISSION to rest. My family and I live near Rocky Mountain National Park and often drive up for a hike and dinner picnic. On a recent trip, we happened upon a mama moose and her calf, only a couple of weeks old. We watched them from a safe distance across the river as they munched on willow branches. After a half hour of foraging, we saw them bed down—the calf curled up next to her mother as they went to sleep.

The more I observe nature, the more I see a freedom to rest. Wildlife follows its God-ordained design of rest without worrying about whether its neighbor moose thinks it is staying busy enough. We, on the other hand, seem to feel as though we need permission to rest or that society might look down on us if we do.

My first real job, at age sixteen, was opening the Panera Bread café at 5:00 a.m. each day. My boss took a deep, frustrated breath when I told him I needed to take every Friday off as a day of rest. Fridays were busy at the restaurant. I wonder now what he, an adult managing a restaurant, thought when a young teenager told him she needed to rest one full day a week. Whatever his thoughts, he granted my request. I spent every Friday exploring local towns and natural areas, reading and journaling in small-town coffee shops, eating good food, and resting. I kept up this Sabbath practice throughout the remainder of high school but gave it up when I entered Bible college. I now find this ironic because of all the places to practice Sabbath, one might think Bible college would be it.

This pattern continued as an ebb and flow of starting and stopping until a few years ago, when my understanding of Sabbath was transformed. I had, at times, viewed Sabbath as a command I grudgingly attempted to obey . . . semi-successfully.

Sound familiar?

Does Sabbath feel ancient and irrelevant or mysterious and intriguing? Perhaps guilt lingers in the air around Sabbath because you've tried and failed in the past. Maybe you are confused about whether it's merely a day off work, a spiritual discipline, or a legalistic command.

But none of those views adequately convey God's original design. Sabbath is a celebration and an invitation to take joy in God and all he has accomplished in and through us throughout the week. It is meant to be fun and freeing. When God hinted at Sabbath on the seventh day of creation, he was giving us permission to stop and delight at least once a week. If you want to infuse life with more meaning, connection, joy, fun, wisdom, and worship, Sabbath carves out space for all that.

What does Sabbath look like in a modern context? Sabbath is for sleeping in, marital intimacy, reading books, journaling, playing outside, doing puzzles, playing chess, knitting, sledding, coffee, hot chocolate, lemonade, laughter, deep conversations, dreaming, thinking, and napping. Remember, God created Sabbath as a gift for you. You won't get it perfect immediately (or ever), so enjoy the process and celebrate the progress. Here are three important first steps:

## 1. Choose a Day and Time

Look at your weekly calendar and identify a chunk of time at least four hours long where you can plug in a Sabbath. Remember, you're not committing to this segment of time forever. Simply find time you can commit to this week. Most weeks my family follows the traditional Hebrew model of celebrating Sabbath from sundown Friday to sundown Saturday. Sunday or a weekday or evening might work better for your schedule. I'm often asked why my family celebrates Sabbath on Friday to Saturday instead of Sunday. We believe fellowship and worshiping with our church family is a vital activity. However, getting four children up, fed, showered, dressed, and to church is not at all restful. We needed a separate time of rest together as a family, so we decided Sabbath would not be on Sunday. Try to choose a day and time when you can truly allow your mind, soul, and body to rest.

## 2. Write a List of Things That Sap Your Energy or Feel Heavy

During your regular week, what feels heavy? What keeps you from hearing God? For most of us, this includes anything to do with screens and media. Write a list of things to remove from your Sabbath day or hours. Consider phones, laptops, news, social media, housework, driving in traffic, and spending money.

A note to parents: This is often where I lose families with babies or young children. Parenthood is ongoing. We are raising the next generation. Diapers need changing, and mouths need to be fed. Arguments need to be worked through. *Don't dismiss Sabbath.* I wrote a specific guide just for you, to share some of our family's practices for Sabbathing with young children. Download it at erynlynum.com /familysabbath.

## 3. Write a List of Things That Fill Your Soul and Energize You

What do you love doing? What inspires you? If you work most of the week at a computer, you might need to do things with your hands and outside on Sabbath, perhaps painting or gardening. If you work as a landscaper or in construction, you might want to sit with a book on Sabbath. Here are some ideas to begin with: gardening, bird-watching, walking, hiking, reading, journaling, playing ball, playing board games, napping, cooking, baking.

But wait. You might be thinking, *Isn't yard work and cooking, well, work?* Be open to new ideas about Sabbath. Sabbath is for us, not us for the Sabbath. If you love cooking but have no time for it during the week, then by all means, buy some fun ingredients and create tasty art in the kitchen on Sabbath. Maybe consider paperware to avoid too many dishes. Work in the garden if you love the feeling of the sun on your skin and dirt beneath your fingernails. But as soon as these feel like work, set them aside. Take a nap. Read a book. If you're struggling to figure out what you enjoy, think about what you did for fun as a kid and start there.

I remember one particular Sabbath when it was gorgeous outside. My husband suggested we work in the yard (often his Sabbath activity of choice on beautiful days). He grabbed branch snippers while I lay in the hammock and fell asleep for three hours. A sunburn I'll never regret.

Make the time. Identify what's heavy and remove it. Focus on what's life-giving, energizing, and inspiring. These are the first steps to embracing God's gift of weekly rest.

### The Roots

So then, there remains a Sabbath rest for the people of God. (Hebrews 4:9)

Remains | ἀπολείπω | *apoleipō* | ap-ol-ipe'-o | to leave behind (leave in place), yet to occur (implying rest is still coming)

Sabbath rest | σαββατισμός | *sabbatismos* | sab-bat-is-mos' | the act of keeping Sabbath (From our study on day 1, remember this Sabbath rest points toward a yet-to-come perfect rest in Christ.)

### Rest & Reflect

At creation God planted a seed of rest and established regular rhythms of retreating and spending time with him—of stopping and delighting in God's presence. Hebrews 4:9 assures us that rest is still available. The seed of rest is neither dormant nor dead. His promise remains, and he means for it to sprout and flourish in your life, making his peace a reality in your everyday activities. If you have viewed Sabbath as an expired tradition, no longer necessary, or unrealistic in today's society, ask God to refresh your perspective. Lay down preconceived notions and feelings of failure, and trust that he will cause the seed of rest to bring forth fruit in your life. Write a prayer below detailing what you hope to experience through Sabbath and surrendering preconceived notions or feelings of past failure.

### Under the Microscope

In week 3 we witnessed Jesus's example of rest in a quiet place (*erēmos*). Jesus also upheld a Sabbath rhythm. Luke 4:16 says, "He came to Nazareth, where he had been brought up. And as was his custom, he went to the synagogue on the Sabbath day, and he stood up to read."

During his ministry, Jesus radically challenged society's perception of Sabbath. He taught as one with authority on the Sabbath and healed on the Sabbath (something the religious establishment considered work). He sought to do away with culture's authoritative and oppressive notions and to highlight God's heart for Sabbath rest. In Mark 2:27–28 he explained, "The Sabbath was made for man, not man for the Sabbath. So the Son of Man is lord even of the Sabbath."

The Sabbath isn't a list of rules we're required to obey as if we were slaves to the idea of work and rest. Sabbath is meant to serve humans, to allow us to live fully alive, as God intended. Without rest we have a partial experience of God. We live half dead, wearily, and even robotically, moving from one activity to the next while compromising vital activities. Make no mistake: Jesus is Lord over the Sabbath and granted it to us as part of his promise for abundant life.

He wrote the guidebook for it.

And on the first page of that guidebook, the dedication reads, "For my child."

He created Sabbath for you.

And you are meant to be free.

Take time today to dream about what an abundant life looks like. Write out a vision for Sabbath and a practice of regular rest. What activities do you want to enjoy? What currently feels heavy—work responsibilities, social commitments, or a never-ending onslaught of emails and text messages—that you long for a break from? And how can you delight with God in his creation and restful presence?

# WEEK 5

## *Day 2*

# PREPARING TO REST

HIBERNATING ANIMALS DO NOT SIMPLY decide one day that it's time to take their long winter nap. Instead, they must carefully select and furnish their winter abode. Some line the walls of their quarters with mud or leaves for insulation. Bald-faced hornets create paper insulation by scraping wood off trees or branches, mixing it with saliva, and creating walls within their hives. These wintering abodes are called *hibernacula.*

A hibernaculum is a refuge. It is a safe place amid an uncertain and sometimes hazardous outside world. It is a retreat for restoration and refueling, and it prepares hibernating animals to succeed and thrive.

Sabbath acts as a hibernaculum for our souls in a barren and sometimes dark society. It is a place of safety and belonging where we can be restored and renewed. But like it does for hibernating animals, it takes time and intentionality to ensure Sabbath is genuinely restful and enjoyable.

Traditionally a weekly observance of Sabbath has required careful preparations. These often included baking the challah bread, precooking meals to avoid meal prep on Sabbath, and cleaning the home. In his book *Christ in the Sabbath*, Rich Robinson explains the excitement and anticipation leading up to Sabbath (Shabbat). Men would get haircuts. Fresh flowers were cut for the table. When *Erev Shabbat* (Sabbath Eve) began at sundown on Friday, white Shabbat candles were lit. Preparation built anticipation, and the excitement was palpable.

I have experienced the same with our family Sabbath. Friday is spent wrapping up work and preparing for rest. As the hours draw nearer to sunset, I feel my soul settling into much-needed rest. Over the past few years, we have experienced well-prepared-for Sabbaths and ones in which our preparations fell short, making them not as restful as they could have been. That said, here are some ways we physically, mentally, and spiritually prepare for a successful Sabbath:

## Prepare Physically

- **Clean:** Everyone pitches in on Friday afternoon to clean the house. This isn't a deep clean, but it simply addresses areas that, left unchecked, will make us feel uncomfortable at home. We tidy up, vacuum, and clean the kitchen.
- **Shop:** I make a grocery run (or schedule a grocery delivery) for anything we need for Sabbath. For us that includes ice cream (a Sabbath Eve tradition), an easy breakfast for the morning (eggs, sausage, cinnamon rolls or sweet bread, fruit), paper plates to avoid dishwashing, and cheeses, sausage, and crackers for a snack board for an easy Saturday lunch. Fresh flowers for the table.

## Prepare Mentally

Preparing mentally for Sabbath is a practice of taking every thought captive (2 Corinthians 10:5). Consider what will mentally block you from enjoying rest, and remove those barriers with the steps below.

- **Wrap up work:** I finish any lingering work projects, including answering pressing emails, so I'm not thinking about them over the weekend. Once finished, I set a Sabbath-away message for my email inbox, which reads

*Thank you for your email. I do not check my inbox Friday evenings through Sundays. I look forward to responding to your message in the new week.*

*Thank you,*
*Eryn*

(You would be surprised by how many comments I get on this away message!)

*Sabbath* comes from *Shabbat*, which can mean to "stop" and "delight." Remember to stop and delight in the work you accomplished this week!

- **Put away screens:** I physically store my laptop away in a closet. This is my cue that it's time to rest. I normally also put my phone away in a drawer.

*A note on phones:* If you have a grown child outside the home or an aging parent, you may need your phone available. Sometimes our kids play with neighbor kids on Sabbath, and I keep my phone available in case the neighbors need to get a hold of us. But as best as I can, I keep it out of sight and mind and only check it occasionally for emergencies. Some phones have a feature called Focus Mode, which allows you to select which phone numbers to allow notifications to come in from, "hiding" the rest of your texts and calls until after Sabbath.

*A note on televisions:* If you have a television in a central living space, consider stowing the remote with laptops, phones, and tablets.

With mental barriers to rest removed, think about what ways you currently need rest. Mentally prepare by considering whether you want rest out in creation, through an inspiring activity like cooking or crafting, or with a good book and a journal.

## Prepare Spiritually

- **Approach prayerfully:** As you approach Sabbath, turn your thoughts to God. Ask him to melt away overwhelm, remove the burden, and help you set aside work and distractions. Tell him what you want to celebrate, and ask him to help you rest in mind, body, and spirit.
- **Gather reading material:** People often ask me, as a busy mom with a business, when I find time to read. I don't. There is no time to be found, only made. I make time to read on Sabbath. I always have a stack of books I am reading through, but I often choose one to focus on for Sabbath. For a while, that was books on Sabbath and biblical rest. Some to begin with (besides the one you're holding now) are *The Ruthless Elimination of Hurry* by John Mark Comer and *24/6* by Matthew Sleeth. You might want an easy and fun fiction read for Sabbath or be longing for time to dive into a deeper work of literature to engage intellectually with. Be sure to have a journal nearby. God tends to stir hearts and inspire ideas on Sabbath.

God created hibernating animals to instinctively prepare for rest, and he has designed us with similar instincts. As you prepare, listen to his Spirit inside you. Consider how you physically, mentally, and spiritually need to rest, and make a plan according to those needs. Remember, God means for Sabbath to be a gift to you. Make the most of his gift by intentionally preparing for and anticipating the good things to come.

## The Roots

This is what the LORD has commanded: "Tomorrow is a day of solemn rest, a holy Sabbath to the LORD; bake what you will bake and boil what you will boil, and all that is left over lay aside to be kept till the morning." (Exodus 16:23)

Lay aside | יָנַח | *yānaḥ* | yaw-nakh'| withhold, to cause to rest, set down, give rest to.

Kept | מִשְׁמֶרֶת | *mišmeret* | mish-mer'-reth | guard, watch, keep, preserve

Notice the careful instructions for handling the prepared food. The Israelites were commanded to "lay aside" extra provisions to be guarded, kept, and preserved for the next day. Imagine if the food were stolen or spoiled—they would have nothing to eat on Sabbath, which would make for a lousy celebration.

### Rest & Reflect

Consider these Hebrew words in light of what God does to and for us with Sabbath. He is laying us aside (*yānaḥ*), or withholding us from the noisy world, and giving us rest. Through Sabbath, he guards, preserves, and keeps watch over us. He keeps (*mišmeret*) us in his restful presence and prepares us for abundant living. In what ways do you need God to free you from the noise of this world and keep watch over your mind and heart? Ask him to use Sabbath as a safeguard for your soul.

### Under the Microscope

When God first instructed the Israelites to practice Sabbath, they faced a real barrier to rest. They were used to gathering food each day. The temptation would be to go and gather on their day of rest, which is what we see them doing in Exodus 16:27: "On the seventh day some of the people went out to gather." They were in a routine of gathering, which posed a challenge to rest.

We can face similar temptations in our pursuit of rest. What regular activities, habits, or cultural expectations might prevent you from rest? Identify those barriers and temptations ahead of time so that when they come via a text message, phone call, or messy area of the house, you have already decided to let those things wait because rest is more important. Rather than allowing your previous routine of work keep you from God's abundant life, allow his rest to become an essential and vital part of your routine. This new routine becomes more natural to us as we align our affections with God's. Many times barriers to rest are the result of distorted affections or us going after what we want in life rather than asking what God wants for us. As you prepare physically, mentally, and spiritually for Sabbath, consider these questions:

- Are you focusing too much on gathering (working)? Why?
  Is it from a place of insecurity, fear, or trying to provide

for your own needs? Ask God to help you trust his provisions and that he will bless your act of faith as you accept his gift of rest.

- Are you working to get ahead or attain material possessions? Ask God to set your mind on things above and to gain an eternal perspective as you spend time resting in his presence.

# WEEK 5

## Day 3

# SABBATH IS A
# VITAL ACTIVITY

WHEN SIN DISRUPTED GOD'S PATTERN of rest, a rewiring of our brains began. We are now inclined to raise an objection to rest. We might think that an entire day, or even a big portion of a day, devoted to rest feels frivolous, perhaps even lazy. If celebration and fun seem unnecessary (although I would argue they are critical), consider rest's life-saving benefits. Rest is not merely a leisurely activity. It is, at times, essential for survival. Consider cosmic lichen.

Earthbound lichen is fascinating on its own. It is a mutualistic relationship between fungi and algae, with each bringing unique benefits. Algae photosynthesize and turn the sun's touch into energy. Fungi create a suitable habitat, collecting water for advantageous growth and expansion. And—get this—lichen has traveled in space. Not on its own, but bound to a Russian satellite orbiting earth to test the lichen's hardiness, which proved impressive. Further, in a facility on earth, scientists exposed lichen to intense extraterrestrial conditions. When exposed to harsh Mars-like conditions, lichen goes dormant, or into a deep restful state. Lichen can remain dormant for months or even years until conditions return to normal, and it can "wake up."

Rest is not frivolous. It is essential to our survival. It is vital. When we're under attack from extreme (maybe even alien or nonnatural) circumstances, and you feel you can't make time for Sabbath, it is probably when you need it most. Let a weekly Sabbath be your cue to retreat. Get with Jesus. Go dormant, heal, recalibrate, and resurface when ready.

Sabbath has proven to be vital in my family. In a season of shock and grief after losing my husband's brother, we missed several Sabbath celebrations in a row while traveling and spending time with family. After a few restless weeks, our eleven-year-old son asked, "Mom, can we Sabbath this weekend?" He was feeling the toll of missing our regular rest. I realized that Sabbath had become essential to our weekly rhythm.

Hear this: Sabbath won't be perfect.

I remember one particular Sabbath that was as close to perfect as we'd ever landed. The house was clean and comfortable. The sun was shining. We slept in, enjoyed a delicious brunch, played games, read books, and spent time together outside. The epitome of restfulness.

The following Sabbath began with a trip to urgent care.

Sabbath is a practice. You will do it really well. Then you won't. It's okay. Keep going. And remember, Sabbath is a celebration! In three years of regular Sabbath practice, we have experienced what I call "Sabbath ruts." We fall into these ruts when we become dogmatic or legalistic about what is or is not a part of Sabbath (when we try to serve Sabbath rather than accepting Sabbath as a gift to us). We can also grow tired or bored of certain Sabbath rhythms, and that is okay. You can refresh your Sabbath practice, add new elements, remove others, and adjust as needed. If your Sabbath practice is tired or you don't know how to begin, start experimenting while keeping God's heart for Sabbath top of mind. Sabbath is

- a gift created for you;
- meant to draw your heart to Jesus and align your affections with his;
- restful, energizing, inspiring, and joyful;
- a time to look back and dream forward; and
- a celebration.

Sabbath is a weekly time to set aside technology, work, and distractions as we remember how to be human. Matthew Sleeth wrote, "Sabbath is not one day of vacation a week. It is part of the most solid and tangible time of life."[1]

Here is how our Sabbath celebration often unfolds:

- Friday evening dinner is easy and celebratory. On the menu is tacos, burgers, or pizza, something we know the kids will eat without fuss. Paper plates make for easy cleanup. We start by toasting with sparkling juice and discussing wins and things we're thankful for from the week. We celebrate what God is doing.
- After dinner, books are read, games are played, lights are low, and screens are away. Eventually, a child asks if it's time for ice cream, and we break out paper bowls, several flavors of sweet, creamy goodness, and sprinkles.
- After the kids go to bed, my husband and I share a glass of wine. The pouring, toasting, and first sip feel like communion. We stay up as late as we want reading, knowing we can sleep late in the morning.
- On Saturday morning we linger in bed, allowing our bodies

the rest they need. The kids are already awake. They have probably made themselves first breakfast. They know not to bother us. (That took practice and training. If you have small children and this seems like a faraway dream, take heart and download our Family Sabbath guide at erynlynum.com/familysabbath.)

- We sit with coffee and crack open books. The kids read or play outside.
- Eventually, someone pops some cinnamon rolls into the oven. Eggs are scrambled, sausage is cooked, and the table is set. We gather around for breakfast (second breakfast for the kids). We pray, feast, and eat as slowly as we want because there is nowhere to be.
- With bellies full, we make our way outside. We might walk the neighborhood to find birds or chat with neighbors. If it's winter, we might take sleds and play in the snow. In summer we might work in the garden, throw the ball for the dog, shoot archery, or sit outside and read.
- The afternoon unfolds however we each want it to. The kids mostly play outside. At some point we might play a board game together or launch an impromptu chess tournament. (Dad usually wins.)
- If anyone gets hungry, snacks are available for grabs. Sabbath is for grazing.
- Around dusk, if we want to go out, we go for a drive to find wildlife (dusk is the golden hour for wildlife spotting) or to find a spot to watch the sunset.
- Dinner is easy, usually leftovers or grilling out. After dinner we might wash dishes or tidy up as we ease out of Sabbath.

If you are accustomed to busy weeks without a stop, Sabbath might initially leave you fidgety and uncomfortable. You might have no idea what to do with yourself. If you have kids, they might feel the same. Don't worry. Keep going.

We are learning to be human again, and shutting down for a time is essential to our survival.

### The Roots

> You shall remember that you were a slave in the land of Egypt, and the LORD your God brought you out from there with a mighty hand and an outstretched arm. Therefore the LORD your God commanded you to keep the Sabbath day. (Deuteronomy 5:15)

Remember | זָכַר | *zākar* | zaw-kar' | recall, call to mind, mindfulness

Brought | יָצָא | *yāṣā'* | yaw-tsaw' | deliver, lead out

Keep | עָשָׂה | *'āśâ* | aw-saw' | prepare, make, observe, celebrate

### Rest & Reflect

The purpose of Sabbath is manifold. It is a celebration and a means of transformation (making us more like Jesus). As we use Sabbath to practice rest like Jesus did, we are stepping into his rhythms and becoming more like Christ. God also meant Sabbath to be a day of remembrance. We might not be in physical slavery like the Israelites were, but what can you reflect on and thank God for freeing you from? What might he be liberating you from right now? Let Sabbath be a bookmark in your week, reminding you to reflect on your freedom in Christ.

### Under the Microscope

Back around 445 BC, restoring the walls of Jerusalem was no small task. It took fifty-two days for Nehemiah and his team to complete the work. This included the physical labor of rebuilding the structure with one hand while simultaneously holding weapons in the other hand as they faced incredible threats. When it was all said and done, over 42,360 people and their servants and animals were gathered from exile. They convened in the square to hear Ezra the scribe read the law of Moses.

Can you imagine that gathering? After exile. Following trauma. Feeling abandoned, forgotten, without a place or community, the people assembled to hear the living and active Word spoken over them. What else could such a day be called but holy, or set apart to God? It was a grand celebration, yet as Ezra spoke, people wept too. The living and active Word cuts to the marrow. Hearing it, the people recognized how far they'd wandered from God. Conviction overwhelmed their senses and crushed their spirits. In Nehemiah 1, Nehemiah acknowledged his and his people's sins before beginning the rebuilding. Now, because of the illuminating truth, sorrow over sin filled their hearts. Nehemiah (along with the priest Ezra and the Levites helping share the Word) responded with God's grace.

Read the leaders' words in Nehemiah 8:9–10: "'This day is holy to the LORD your God; do not mourn or weep.' For all the people wept as they heard the words of the Law. Then he said to them, 'Go your way. Eat the fat and drink sweet wine and send portions to anyone who has nothing ready, for this day is holy to our Lord. And do not be grieved, for the joy of the LORD is your strength.'"

Like the Sabbath, God declared the day holy (something set apart and different from other days) and then told the people to rejoice. Embrace joy *because* it's a holy day.

It's not a BYOJ (bring your own joy) situation either. The joy of the Lord is ours for the taking.

With this in mind, it's not a surprise joy is actually commanded on Shabbat in the traditional Hebrew setting. *Oneg Shabbat* refers to the general enjoyment of Shabbat or Sabbath. Holy days are joyous, a remembrance of where that joy wells up from: God himself, whose joy is our strength.

Sabbath might bring up unexpected emotions, like when the assembled people wept at God's words. Stepping into rest allows space for introspection and reflection, which can bring up feelings of guilt or shame, or on the opposite spectrum, joy and delight. In fact, like the people at Jerusalem, we might need to go through some time of repentance, or turning away from our own ways and toward God, so we can access the joy of Sabbath. Ask God to prepare you for whatever insights and emotions Sabbath might bring to the surface, and ask him to help you access his delight and joy made available through rest.

# WEEK 5

## Day 4

# GOD'S PROVISION
# FOR SABBATH

RIGHT BEFORE GOD ESTABLISHED SABBATH in Exodus 16:23 (the first mention of Sabbath in Scripture), he gave the Israelites manna to satisfy their grumbling stomachs. Can you imagine if God had asked them to trust him by resting one day a week when they were still suffering from hunger pangs? It would not have gone well. But the story of the manna shows exactly how God works: God prepares us and gives us what we need to trust him.

There are many thoughts and opinions as to what manna might have been. Some scholars have noted that certain trees in Palestine produce a substance similar to the Bible's description of manna. However, we must be careful not to over-naturalize manna or constrain it to a biological box. Indeed, God could have used something he'd fashioned in creation. Still, it's also not beyond him to perform a miracle beyond the natural laws he put into place. Whatever it was or wasn't, manna *was* a miraculous provision. And what I love is that God used moisture to produce it. Scripture mentions both rain and dew.

We see a similar effect with mushrooms.

Mushrooms are not random, individual fungal entities popping up wherever they want. Instead, they are the fruiting bodies of a much more elaborate and unseen underground mycorrhizal network made up of tiny threads called *hyphae*. It's a sophisticated system that holds much of nature together. What makes a mushroom pop up from the ground overnight? Moisture. Mushrooms require moisture to activate and grow. When a fresh mushroom pops up from the soil, it is evidence of the vast living network of hyphae below it.

Consider this in light of manna's description. In Exodus 16:4 God promised Moses, "Behold, I am about to rain bread from heaven for you," and in verses 13–14 we read, "In the morning dew lay around the camp. And when the dew had gone up, there was on the face of the wilderness a fine, flake-like thing, fine as frost on the ground."

Sometimes God's provision is right beneath the surface, present but unseen, waiting for his cue. Like a mushroom appearing in the morning, we can learn to spot God's blessings and know there's much more beneath the surface than we can see.

God is still raining down blessings today, and it very likely won't look like you expect it to. James 1:17 says, "Every good gift and every perfect gift is from above, coming down from the Father of lights, with whom there is no variation or shadow due to change."

I laugh each time I picture the Israelites walking outside that first morning. The ground was covered in a flaky, bread-like . . . thing. Read their comical response in verse 15: "When the people of Israel saw it, they said to one another, 'What is it?' For they did not know what it was." I envision Moses dumbfounded at their confusion as he responded, "It is the bread that the LORD has given you to eat."

*Uh . . . guys, it's that thing you asked for.*

When I'm overwhelmed and burned out, God points to rest and says the same thing Moses said to the Israelites: "It's that thing you asked for."

My response to rest used to reflect the Israelites' reaction to bread on that first morning. Rest doesn't look how I expected it to. *What is it?* I asked.

You might be asking the same.

I certainly didn't see rest as God's answer to my requests for more peace, a settled mind, or wisdom. Yet his gift of rest makes space for all these. As I rest, I receive his blessings. Without rest, I often miss them.

If Sabbath, or in a broader sense, rest, looks foreign and unfamiliar—like morning manna—that's okay. Lean in. Take a risk. Try something new.

Rest might not be what you expect, but it is God's miracle and provision you need.

### The Roots

> They spoke against God, saying,
> "Can God spread a table in the wilderness?"
> (Psalm 78:19)

Spread | עָרַךְ | *ʿāraḵ* | aw-rak' | furnish, prepare

Table | שֻׁלְחָן | *šulḥān* | shool-khawn' | for personal or sacred use, implies a meal

Wilderness | מִדְבָּר | *miḏbār* | mid-bawr' | desert, open land

### Rest & Reflect

It has been argued that when the Israelites grumbled against Moses and Aaron, they weren't *actually* starving. It was like when a child reports they are starving because they can't find their favorite snack in the pantry. Psalm 78:18 says the Israelites tested God "by demanding the food they craved." They had a craving. In their doubt—perhaps mockingly—they asked whether God could spread a table in the wilderness.

Maybe in our hunger for more peace, we're asking for the wrong things or looking in the wrong places for what we crave rather than what will truly satisfy.

Let's ask for peace and rest with bold and unrestrained confidence, in line with God's Word and what he wants for us. If you're in the wilderness, say out loud, "I trust that God can spread a table for me." Psalm 78:25 says God "sent them food in abundance," and in verse 29 that "they ate and were well filled."

Let Sabbath be a table of peace and abundant life spread for you in the wilderness. It might not look exactly as you imagined, but it will be what you need. Ask God with bold confidence to bless you through his gift of rest. Come, eat, be filled.

### Under the Microscope

Reading the miracle of manna in Exodus 16, God makes something abundantly clear: Manna is temporary. It spoils. It's supermarket deli sushi, so don't trust it the next day (unless it's the seventh day—we'll get to that tomorrow). God instructed the Israelites not to leave any manna overnight. When they did, it rotted and was infested with worms. Likely, God designed manna to quickly spoil for two reasons:

1. To teach Israel to trust his daily provision (new morning mercies, grace upon grace, give us this day our daily bread).

2. To point forward to Jesus, the eternal bread that never spoils. Manna is referenced three times in the New Testament, most prominently in John 6. In this chapter, the miracle of manna comes full circle and to completion. After Jesus performed a miracle and fed a crowd of over five thousand by multiplying five loaves and two fish, the people put Jesus to the test. How was he any better than Moses, who had also produced bread? Read Jesus's response in verses 26–35 and answer the questions below.

## JOHN 6:26-35

[26] Jesus answered them, "Truly, truly, I say to you, you are seeking me, not because you saw signs, but because you ate your fill of the loaves. [27] Do not work for the food that perishes, but for the food that endures to eternal life, which the Son of Man will give to you. For on him God the Father has set his seal." [28] Then they said to him, "What must we do, to be doing the works of God?" [29] Jesus answered them, "This is the work of God, that you believe in him whom he has sent." [30] So they said to him, "Then what sign do you do, that we may see and believe you? What work do you perform? [31] Our fathers ate the manna in the wilderness; as it is written, 'He gave them bread from heaven to eat.'" [32] Jesus then said to them, "Truly, truly, I say to you, it was not Moses who gave you the bread from heaven, but my Father gives you the true bread from heaven. [33] For the bread of God is he who comes down from heaven and gives life to the world." [34] They said to him, "Sir, give us this bread always."

[35] Jesus said to them, "I am the bread of life; whoever comes to me shall not hunger, and whoever believes in me shall never thirst."

- Why were the people seeking Christ? Were their motives pure? Selfish? Narrow-minded? (v. 26) How do you approach God with your requests?
- Notice how Jesus shifts their perspective from temporal provisions to eternal sustenance in verse 27. This is an aha moment where we realize, *Oh! Manna points forward to Jesus!* It is stunning. In what areas might God want to reroute your attention away from things that spoil and toward what is lasting?
- What does Jesus tell them to do to partake in God's work (v. 29)? How can you believe and rest as a part of God's important purpose for your life? How might knowing that God provides every morning help you continue moving forward?
- Repeat the peoples' request to Jesus: "Give us this bread always." Jesus's presence is our sustenance. Ask him for daily bread in the form of rest.

# WEEK 5

## Day 5

# SABBATH IS AN ACT OF FAITH

GOD DESIGNED MANY BIRDS TO survive and thrive through a strategy called *scatter hoarding*. Scatter hoarding is when a creature gathers and stores caches of food in numerous areas, which it uses throughout cold months when food is more difficult to find. The champion scatter hoarder is the Clark's nutcracker. This bird can collect over thirty seeds every minute, storing up to one hundred in pouches beneath its tongue. Using this strategy, an individual Clark's nutcracker can hide around a hundred thousand seeds each year, across a twenty-mile radius. Perhaps more incredible than their ability to gather and store seeds is their memory for locating their caches when they need them. A single bird can create up to twenty-thousand cache sites a year and remember where almost all of them are. Thankfully, when God called the Israelites to gather manna, they only needed to keep track of it for one day.

When God provided the Israelites with manna, he wasn't only delivering physical sustenance. He also had a powerful lesson and gift that would satisfy far more than their stomachs. Notice his specific instructions for the sixth and seventh days in Exodus 16:5: "On the sixth day, when they prepare what they bring in, it will be twice as much as they gather daily." In verses 22–23, we see the Israelites gathering two portions:

> On the sixth day they gathered twice as much bread, two omers each. And when all the leaders of the congregation came and told Moses, he said to them, "This is what the LORD has commanded: 'Tomorrow is a day of solemn rest, a holy Sabbath to the LORD; bake what you will bake and boil what you will boil, and all that is left over lay aside to be kept till the morning.'"

On each day, God provided an omer, or portion, for each person (v. 16). On the sixth day, God provided two omers, a double portion, so they would not need to gather on the seventh day. Think about this: The Israelites had minimal context for what God was telling them to do. Indeed, they could think back to God resting on the seventh day, but verse 23 is the Bible's first mention of Sabbath. With no real context, resting and observing Sabbath required a huge amount of faith in God for the Israelites. The people had to trust him for the seventh day. Make no mistake—Sabbath and rest are an act of faith.

On this first Sabbath, God established the framework for the rest he created on the seventh day of creation. Work six days, then stop. And he was serious about stopping. Notice what happened when some failed to obey and stop in verses 27–29:

> On the seventh day some of the people went out to gather, but they found none. And the LORD said to Moses, "How long will you refuse to keep my commandments and my laws? See! The LORD has given you the Sabbath; therefore on the sixth day he gives you bread for two days. Remain

each of you in his place; let no one go out of his place on the seventh day."

How often do you and I try to gather on that seventh day? *Just one more project. A few more emails. Bills need to be paid. We need to hustle.*

The Enemy whispers lies to keep us from resting. He will do whatever he can to get us out on that seventh day, trying to gather just a little more. And yet our lack of faith destroys the peace God intends for us. In our tireless pursuits to gather, create, build, or get just one more thing done, we forfeit God's gift of abundant life through rest.

Three years ago I knew that if our family was going to practice Sabbath, I had to trust God with the seventh day. And you know what happened? He showed up with abundance. Our workweeks are more productive. We have more focus and energy. I am more creative and energized. Notice the keyword *more.* When we surrender our exhausting pursuit of more (more tasks, more progress, more money, more work, more acknowledgment), God gives us more—more blessings, more life, more perspective, more joy, more of him.

Of course, celebrating Sabbath will undoubtedly mean there are some things we don't get to each week. But think back to the analogy of the jar on day 4 of week 4, with rocks representing our values or vital activities, and sand representing the smaller, less significant things in life. Sabbath carves out space for what truly matters and helps us recognize that some of the things we don't get to simply don't need to be gotten to. When we place the rocks of rest, family times, faith, joy, and worship into the jar, there is less time, or no time, for the things we don't actually need to give our time to.

Take a measured risk. Trust God's math. Gather up his gift of rest. It is more than sufficient.

Identify areas where you are trying to force results or to gather when you should be resting. Ask God to help you develop discernment for when enough is enough. Ask him to help you know when to stop and delight in what he's allowed you to accomplish rather than trying to push that accomplishment outside his life-giving bounds.

## The Roots

> And God is able to make all grace abound to you, so that having all sufficiency in all things at all times, you may abound in every good work. (2 Corinthians 9:8)

Grace | χάρις | *charis* | khar'-ece | goodwill, loving-kindness, favor, bounty, delight

Abound | περισσεύω | *perisseuō* | per-is-syoo'-o | to make an abundance, to overflow, to excel, to exceed

Sufficiency | αὐτάρκεια | *autarkeia* | ow-tar'-ki-ah | contentment

## Rest & Reflect

What often keeps us from Sabbath rest is a sense that there is simply too much to do to take a break. What if we changed our idea of Sabbath away from taking a break and instead viewed it as an essential element of our work? What might happen if we view rest as a vital activity that infuses our experiences with more life? God provides abundantly for us when we follow his plan. He gives a double portion. We only need to accept his gift to rest contentedly in his provisions, knowing that he provides all we need for every good work. Ask God to give you a double portion of faith to trust his Sabbath math.

If you have concerns over taking time to rest, journal honestly about them below and surrender your hesitancy to God.

### Under the Microscope

Regularly celebrating Sabbath circles us back to God's presence. Although spiritually we should grow more aware of his presence each day, Sabbath is a built-in training course in practicing the presence of God. Matthew Sleeth wrote, "Observing a Sabbath ensures that at the very worst, we are never more than six days away from a holy perspective."[1]

Read Psalm 84:10–12 below. Consider how it relates to today's lesson on trusting God for his abundant provisions. Then answer the questions.

## PSALM 84:10–12

[10] For a day in your courts is better
   than a thousand elsewhere.
I would rather be a doorkeeper in the house of my God
   than dwell in the tents of wickedness.
[11] For the LORD God is a sun and shield;
   the LORD bestows favor and honor.
No good thing does he withhold
   from those who walk uprightly.
[12] O LORD of hosts,
   blessed is the one who trusts in you!

- Can you picture Sabbath becoming your favorite day of the week, better than "a thousand elsewhere" (v. 10)? What would need to be true in your Sabbath practice for it to be a day of joy, celebration, and rest?

- How might Sabbath help you see God as a sun (sustenance, warmth, light, energy) and a shield (protection) (v. 11)?

- What "good things" do you long for God to make available through your practice of Sabbath? Ask him to help you richly receive his abundant blessings as you rest expectantly in his presence, and then thank him in anticipation of his perfectly timed, perfectly unique provision.

- How might Sabbath help you be one who walks uprightly? How does the holiness, or set-apart nature of the Sabbath, help us live more like Christ?

- What specifically do you need to trust God with as you step into or refresh your Sabbath practice (v. 12)?

# WEEK 5

*Days 6 and 7*

# STOP & DELIGHT

## ENVISION SABBATH

TAKE TIME TO DREAM ABOUT what Sabbath can look like in your life. After a few years of celebrating Sabbath, I still do this. As life changes, I might need to experience rest in new ways. My family and I check in with our Sabbath practice and adjust as needed. Our first year was extreme. Almost every Saturday, we stayed home and did not drive anywhere. After a year of that, we were missing our time exploring and hiking as a family, so we adjusted, and if we want to hike or explore, we are free to do that on Sabbath.

Write down your dreams for Sabbath. How do you want to experience God? What do you hope to see happen in your family? What do you want more time for? Don't hold back. Dream big. Since the garden of Eden, God has meant for Sabbath to be a blessing in your life and for rest to be a regular rhythm of your week.

### Journaling Questions

Have you tried practicing Sabbath before? What was your experience? Do you have any guilt or feelings of failure around Sabbath?

Surrender your past experiences to God and ask him to refresh your perspective on his gift of rest.

In what ways can you practically prepare for Sabbath? Begin making a list of ways you can prepare physically, mentally, and spiritually.

How can you remove temptation to accomplish *one more thing* in your week, and instead trust God for a day of rest? How can you wrap up work and responsibilities and put away any temptation that would disrupt your rest?

# WEEK 6

## ABIDE
## Living at Rest

*Abide in me, and I in you. As the branch cannot bear fruit by itself, unless it abides in the vine, neither can you, unless you abide in me.*

JOHN 15:4

# WEEK 6

## *Day 1*

# A PRACTICE IN STAYING

BIRDS DON'T DELAY DURING MIGRATION journeys as they make their way across vast stretches of land and sea. Arriving at their breeding or feeding grounds in good time is imperative to their survival. Yet sometimes they have to stop and wait. If inclement weather rolls in, birds must find a safe spot to land and wait it out until they can continue on their way. These unplanned rest stops are called *fallouts*.

Like a bird following a migratory pathway, I can often become hyper-focused on where I'm going or what I want to accomplish in life. While keen focus can help us remain faithful to what God has called us to, if we're not careful, it can also prevent us from seeing when conditions are unsafe to continue. Birds don't plan to encounter spring snow or thunderstorms. We don't plan for sickness, exhaustion, tragedy, or other disruptions to our plans. But like taking shelter to wait out a storm, stopping, staying, and resting are critical if we want to continue on our way once conditions have settled. Stopping and staying helps us live less reactively and more intentionally.

Consider if a bird threw caution to the wind and decided to continue in a storm. It might use up critical energy reserves and never make its destination. That's what burnout looks like. Rather than making frantic decisions and reroutes or trying to regain control of circumstances outside our grasp, we can stop, catch our breath, and choose to remain in God's restful presence. God is our fallout, a safe place to stop and rest before continuing on.

Scripture uses a beautiful word for staying: *abide*, or the Greek word μένω (*menō*), which is also translated as "remaining" and "dwelling." We find this idea of abiding deeply connected to the concept of rest. Dwell for a moment on the first words of John 15:4: "Abide in me, and I in you." As we abide (*menō*), remain, and dwell in Christ, Christ abides in us. We have the restful presence of Jesus Christ dwelling inside us. How might Christ residing in us affect our countenance and presence? How might his restful presence adjust our pace and guide us back into God's pattern of rest? Abiding in Christ aligns us with his heart for rest.

John Piper says, "Abide means not ceasing to rest in [Scripture's] *grace* and *power*—never turning away as though greater peace could be found anywhere else."[1]

This week, we will explore the practice of abiding in John 15 and corresponding passages. As we study, consider these questions:

- What unexpected circumstances are disrupting your plans?
- Is God asking you to stop, stay, and rest awhile before continuing on?
- How might God want to strengthen and prepare you for the way ahead as you abide in him?

Think about the birds fixated on their migration journeys. This is how we often continue through our days, always focusing on progress. But what if forward motion is made possible through regular rest?

Rest is a profound means of spiritual growth. As we practice resting, we are learning to abide—to dwell in God's restful presence—even when it isn't comfortable.

## The Roots

Abide in me, and I in you. As the branch cannot bear fruit by itself, unless it abides in the vine, neither can you, unless you abide in me. (John 15:4)

Abide | μένω | *menō* | men'-o | remain, dwell, continue, endure

Branch | κλῆμα | *klēma* | klay'-mah | a tender and flexible branch, vine sprout

## Rest & Reflect

Do you remember the theme of our first week of study? We focused on *returning* to a pattern of rest. On the first day of our final week, it seems fitting to focus on the concept of *remaining*. Once we return to God's rest, we need to practice staying connected to the one person who supplies us with strength and peace. Sometimes staying is the hardest thing to do. Our minds wander. We become antsy. We fidget. Remember that each time we practice returning and remaining in God's rest, the easier it becomes. This is a practice of remaining in God's restful presence, or abiding. Write a prayer asking God to help you become comfortable with staying. Ask him to remove tendencies toward rush and distraction—name those specific tendencies below—and to show you the power of abiding in his restful presence.

## *Under the Microscope*
Read John 15:1–17 below.

- Circle every instance of *abide*.
- Underline every reference to belief or unbelief.

We will be studying this passage in the following days, so mark up the text, write questions in the margins, and highlight repeated words or ideas.

## JOHN 15:1–17

[1] I am the true vine, and my Father is the vinedresser. [2] Every branch in me that does not bear fruit he takes away, and every branch that does bear fruit he prunes, that it may bear more fruit. [3] Already you are clean because of the word that I have spoken to you. [4] Abide in me, and I in you. As the branch cannot bear fruit by itself, unless it abides in the vine, neither can you, unless you abide in me. [5] I am the vine; you are the branches. Whoever abides in me and I in him, he it is that bears much fruit, for apart from me you can do nothing. [6] If anyone does not abide in me he is thrown away like a branch and withers; and the branches are gathered, thrown into the fire, and burned. [7] If you abide in me, and my words abide in you, ask whatever you wish, and it will be done for you. [8] By this my Father is glorified, that you bear much fruit and so prove to be my disciples. [9] As the Father has loved me, so have I loved you. Abide in my love. [10] If you keep my commandments, you will abide in my love, just as I have kept my Father's commandments and abide in his love. [11] These things I have spoken to you, that my joy may be in you, and that your joy may be full.

[12] This is my commandment, that you love one another as I have loved you. [13] Greater love has no one than this, that someone lay down his life for his friends. [14] You are my friends if you do what I command you. [15] No longer do I call you servants, for the servant does not know what his master is doing; but I have called you friends, for all that I have heard from my Father I have made known to you. [16] You did not choose me, but I chose you and appointed you that you should go and bear fruit and that your fruit should abide, so that whatever you ask the Father in my name, he may give it to you. [17] These things I command you, so that you will love one another.

As you practice resting and establishing a regular rhythm through Sabbath, consider how you can remain in God's rest. What old habits or temptations might cause you to slip back into frenzied living or an unsustainable pace? Write down a few ways you can proactively remain in God's restful presence.

## WEEK 6

*Day 2*

# GOD'S RESTFUL PRESENCE GOES WITH YOU

THE FIRST TIME I SAW bighorn sheep in the wild, they had lambs. I watched in awe as these large yet agile animals led their young across the jutting edges of the Rocky Mountains. Bighorn sheep escape predators by maneuvering nearly impossible rock faces, sometimes balancing on ledges only a couple of inches wide. Within an hour of birth, lambs are nearly as strong and dexterous as adults and follow their mothers and the herd to restful places amid impressively difficult conditions.

In the Old Testament, Moses found himself facing an arduous path ahead. When God told Moses to lead the Israelites away from Mount Sinai and to the promised land, there was one big problem: God told them he would not be going with them. He promised to send an angel before them to drive out their enemies, but in Exodus 33:3 he added, "But I will not go up among you, lest I consume you on the way, for you are a stiff-necked people." Their rebellion threatened their ability to have God's presence go with them.

Verse 4 says, "When the people heard this disastrous word, they mourned." To not have God present with them along the journey would be catastrophic. Picture a young bighorn sheep without its mother and herd to guide it. Upon hearing this terrible news, Moses took action. Verses 12–17 detail a beautiful interaction between God and Moses where Moses intercedes on behalf of the people. Verse 12 begins, "See, you say to me, 'Bring up this people,' but you have not let me know whom you will send with me."

*How can we ever do this alone, God?*

Have you asked the same question? Have you doubted God's presence and feared that you're navigating life, or at least stretches of it, solo?

Moses and the Israelites couldn't stay put.

Bighorn sheep must continue and move and find food, water, and shelter.

Migrating birds, after an unexpected fallout and rest, must continue on their way.

And we can't live forever in *erēmos*, the quiet place, or Sabbath.

So how do we live restfully while not in a place set apart for rest? How can we remain at rest as we move through our days?

We can learn from Moses's response. When God withheld his presence because of the people's rebellion, Moses boldly brought his concern to God, asking him to "show me now your ways, that I may know you in order to find favor in your sight. Consider too that this nation is your people" (v. 13). *Yes, we are rebellious. Show me your ways, then. Correct me. Make me favorable. Consider these, your children . . .*

In essence, Moses's next step was to ask God to fix up his people so he could go with them.

How does God respond? With grace: "My presence will go with you, and I will give you rest" (v. 14).

What would bring the people rest? God's presence.

The same is true for us, and we access God's presence through his Holy Spirit. Because Jesus came to earth to dwell physically with us, we can always have God's Spirit inside us:

And the Word [Christ] became flesh and dwelt among us, and we have seen his glory, glory as of the only Son from the Father, full of grace and truth. (John 1:14)

I tell you the truth: it is to your advantage that I go away, for if I do not go away, the Helper will not come to you. But if I go, I will send him to you. (16:7)

Do you find yourself asking the same question Moses did? *God, can you just fix me up? Make me worthy of your presence? What must I do?*

This question is answered in the blood of Christ. As believers, we have full access to God, for Christ has made us worthy. As Hebrews 4:16 says, "Let us then with confidence draw near to the throne of grace, that we may receive mercy and find grace to help in time of need."

When we cannot withdraw to a quiet place, God can quiet our souls merely by his proximity. His presence goes with us into rush-hour traffic, school drop-offs and pickups, the cubicle or office, the grocery store, and the doctor's office. When circumstances outside of us threaten the peace within us, we can remember God is our ever-present help in trouble (Psalm 46:1). When you feel your shoulders tighten and stress or anxiety rising, take a deep breath and pray: *Lord, your presence goes with me. Go before me now and help me rest with your presence abiding inside me.*

God never leaves us to navigate the way on our own. Instead, his presence goes with us and gives us rest.

### The Roots

My presence will go with you, and I will give you rest. (Exodus 33:14)

Presence | פָּנִים | *pānîm* | paw-neem' | face, person, before (position)

Rest | נוּחַ | *nûaḥ* | noo'-akh | settle down, be quiet, granted rest

### Rest & Reflect

The *pānîm*, or person, or very presence of God the Holy Spirit, is inside of every believer. Think about the potential of this. God's thoughts, affections, and wisdom dwell inside our spirits. As we allow him to settle us, quiet our minds, and grant us rest, we can better discern what his Spirit is saying and doing inside us. Because the Spirit is with us, not only do we have a way back to the original pattern of vital rest and vital work but God himself is restoring us and imparting life. Are you currently facing stressful conditions or an upcoming busy season you're concerned about? Ask God for his restful presence to lead you through. Name the specific things you are concerned about—perhaps lack of time, energy, focus, or patience. Ask him to powerfully guide you through and keep your mind and soul at rest along the way.

### Under the Microscope

Jesus is our direct connection to the trinity (God the Father, God the Son, and God the Holy Spirit). He is our access to God's presence.

WEEK 6 | *Day 2*

Read John 14:8–12 and follow the steps below, then answer the questions:

- Circle *enough* in verse 8 and draw a line from it to *Whoever has seen me has seen the Father.* Write in the margin "Jesus is our access to God's restful presence."
- Underline *I am in the Father and the Father is in me* in verse 10. Next to it, write "The Father is in Jesus, and Jesus is in me. God's restful presence dwells inside me."

## JOHN 14:8–12

[8] Philip said to him, "Lord, show us the Father, and it is enough for us." [9] Jesus said to him, "Have I been with you so long, and you still do not know me, Philip? Whoever has seen me has seen the Father. How can you say, 'Show us the Father'? [10] Do you not believe that I am in the Father and the Father is in me? The words that I say to you I do not speak on my own authority, but the Father who dwells in me does his works. [11] Believe me that I am in the Father and the Father is in me, or else believe on account of the works themselves.

[12] "Truly, truly, I say to you, whoever believes in me will also do the works that I do; and greater works than these will he do, because I am going to the Father."

- Have you ever felt like Philip, desiring to experience God and see him more clearly? Consider Jesus's response: "Have I been with you so long, and you still do not know me, Philip?" (v. 9). Is Jesus saying the same to you? He is readily available and eager to reveal himself to you if you ask.

- What is your initial reaction when you read that we will do the same works as Christ, as co-laborers with him (v. 12)?
- What works are you longing for God to perform in and through you?

Surrender those desires to him, asking him to align your aspirations with his and to do a mighty work inside you that will become an outpouring of his power and love to those around you. It all begins with abiding, so ask him to teach you to abide well.

# WEEK 6

*Day 3*

# RESTFUL WATERS

STAGNANT WATER MIGHT BE GOOD for the fairy shrimp in vernal pools, like we learned about in week 3, but it's not great for other wildlife. Still or standing water is vulnerable to contamination, toxicity, and spoiling. So when we read Psalm 23:2, "He leads me beside still waters," a sour, bubbly, slimy green pond is not likely what the psalmist had in mind.

The Hebrew word used in Psalm 23:2 for *still* is most often translated as "rest" *or* "resting." When we read "still waters," it is helpful to remember the imagery is not of stagnant water but of a calm, cascading spring that brings the fresh influx of water essential to its ecosystem and the creatures and plants that call it home.

Jesus, who is often called the Good Shepherd, talked about life-giving water in John 4:14: "Whoever drinks of the water that I will give him will never be thirsty again. The water that I will give him will become in him a spring of water welling up to eternal life." This isn't physical water Jesus was talking about. Instead, he was addressing our needs that run deeper than physical sustenance. His living water refreshes our souls. In that chapter Jesus was telling a woman at the well that she needed his truth and life in her soul more than water in her bucket.

We can run ourselves weary by chasing water to fill our buckets—pursuing things we think we need or want, whether a better financial situation, relationship, career, accolades, influence, reputation, or comfort. But the solution to our thirst is right in front of us.

Notice that the statement in Psalm 23:1, "The LORD is my shepherd," is followed by "I shall not want." Verse 2 continues, "He makes me lie down in green pastures. He leads me beside still waters." When we trust God's provisions and discover contentment in his presence, not only are we freed from a gnawing desire for more, but we can rest, trusting that he is leading us to a place where we can thrive in the same way nature thrives near a calm spring of water.

As we abide in God's presence and partake of his living, restful waters, we are freed from the torrential current of want.

Try this practice—as you read through Psalm 23 below, insert "I shall not want" on the blank lines after each statement:

The LORD is my shepherd; I shall not want.
He makes me lie down in green pastures.

_____.


He leads me beside still waters.
He restores my soul.

_____.


He leads me in paths of righteousness
for his name's sake.

_____.

Even though I walk through the valley of the shadow of
    death,
    I will fear no evil,
for you are with me;
    your rod and your staff,
    they comfort me.

You prepare a table before me
    in the presence of my enemies;

you anoint my head with oil;
    my cup overflows.

Surely goodness and mercy shall follow me
    all the days of my life,

and I shall dwell in the house of the LORD
    forever.

A great way to add selah pauses to your day, which also remind you of God's still-water presence, is to memorize Psalm 23 with this repetition of *I shall not want.* Sit and recite the words first thing in the morning until your soul internalizes them. Experience freedom from entangling want at the front end of the day.

What makes a content and restful life possible? God's presence. We can rest because he makes us lie down in green pastures, a picture of provision and abundance. We can rest because whatever life looks like, God leads us beside still, restful waters. We can rest because he restores our souls. We can rest because he leads us in paths of righteousness for his name's sake.

God's restful presence—as experienced through Sabbath, selah moments, and in *erēmos* (the quiet place)—is restful waters. We are regularly restored by remaining near and never veering far from them.

Has the path you are on taken you far away from restful waters? Are you struggling to experience God's restful presence? Internalize Psalm 23 this week. Try to come to it with a fresh perspective. Write it on a card and hang it from your bathroom mirror. Listen to it. Read it in a different translation. Picture restful waters in your spirit, or aloud repeat "I shall not want. I don't need to want. Christ in me is sufficient. He makes me lie down in green pastures. He leads me beside still waters."

### The Roots

> He leads me beside still waters.
> He restores my soul.
> (Psalm 23:2–3)

Leads | נָהַל | *nāhal* | naw-hal'| led to water or resting place, refresh

Still | מְנוּחָה | *mᵊnûḥâ* | men-oo-khaw' | rest, resting place, quiet

Restores | שׁוּב | *šûḇ* | shoob | turn back to God, return

## Rest & Reflect

The word translated as *restore* carries a theme of repentance and being made right with God. We can be made right with God through Jesus's blood and have an eternal future secured in God's presence. We can also experience a regular return to God's rest in our daily lives, but at times, accessing that rest first requires repentance, or turning away from wrongdoing and ill-advised choices and back to God's way.

Is there any instance of rush, frenzy, or wandering away from God's pace and plan that you want to acknowledge before him? Take this opportunity to repent and turn back from your own way or unsustainable pace, return to God's restful presence, and be restored.

## Under the Microscope

In John 4 Jesus encountered a woman at the well who, as we glean insight into her story, must have been restless—not only physically from regularly walking to the well, drawing up, and carrying water, but spiritually, as she was living in sin and estranged from God's presence (John 4:16–18). Yet here at the well, she met the very presence of God through Jesus Christ. Do you think she could sense his restful presence? Perhaps that's what intrigued her to carry on conversation with a stranger. Follow their dialogue in John 4:10–14 below and follow these steps, then answer the questions:

- Underline *gift of God*. Write any ideas you have of what this might have meant. Could it allude to God's presence, truth, and peace?
- In the passage, differentiate between physical water and living, spiritual water.

  - Write "P" for *physical* above any mentions of water coming from the well or for physical thirst.
  - Write "S" for *spiritual* above any mentions of living water or water that ultimately satisfies.

## JOHN 4:10–14

[10] Jesus answered her, "If you knew the gift of God, and who it is that is saying to you, 'Give me a drink,' you would have asked him, and he would have given you living water." [11] The woman said to him, "Sir, you have nothing to draw water with, and the well is deep. Where do you get that living water? [12] Are you greater than our father Jacob? He gave us the well and drank from it himself, as did his sons and his livestock." [13] Jesus said to her, "Everyone who drinks of this water will be thirsty again, [14] but whoever drinks of the water that I will give him will never be thirsty again. The water that I will give him will become in him a spring of water welling up to eternal life." [15] The woman said to him, "Sir, give me this water, so that I will not be thirsty or have to come here to draw water."

- Are you chasing after anything more eagerly than you're pursuing Christ? In what areas are you looking for satisfaction outside of Christ? Surrender those desires to God and ask him to change your affections and aspirations to align with his plan and purpose. Ask him to help you experience deep satisfaction in his restful presence.

- Have you experienced "water welling up to eternal life" (v. 14)?" If so, what do you remember from that time? Eternal security and rest only come through Jesus Christ. If you have never trusted him to fully satisfy and save you, do so today.

- Be bold like the woman at the well and ask Jesus to give you living water and to help you daily experience the gift of God mentioned in verse 10. Ask him to lead you to restful, life-giving waters every day as you seek his presence and truth.

# WEEK 6

## Day 4

# RESTFUL RESULTS

Vinedressers understand how crucial rest is for producing a good crop. Grape plants experience a pause of growth called a *lag phase*. This pause can last one to three weeks, depending on the variety. During this time, fruit stops growing, but the plant is not idle. This is an essential stage in seed development. In fact, if the fruit continues its productive pursuit of growth and never pauses, the seeds will not develop properly. After this critical pause, the berries soften and gain color.

In a similar way, the quality and effectiveness of our work relies on rest periods. If we press on without pausing, we miss important growth stages. Both our inward work (our spiritual transformation to look more like Christ) and our outward work (the tasks God has given us) can be stunted.

Scripture calls the results of our work, or the good things we produce for God's kingdom, fruit. And like with a grapevine, rest is critical for our fruit. We can see this connection in John 15, which we studied earlier this week. On the first day of this week, you circled every mention of *abide* in John 15:1–17. Flip back to that page and count how many times abide is used in the text. You should find eleven. The first ten mentions are bunched together in verses 4–10. Here are three ways *abide* is used in them:

- We abide in Christ and Christ abides in us (vv. 4–5).
- Christ's word abides in us (v. 7; see also Colossians 3:16).
- We abide in Christ's love. Christ abides in God's love (v. 10).

There is one more mention of abide in verse 16—but this one is different. It is set apart. It does not directly address us, Christ, God, or the Word (God's truth) abiding. Instead, it is *our fruit*, or the product of our work and efforts, that abides. Read the text: "You did not choose me, but I chose you and appointed you that you should go and bear fruit and that your *fruit should abide*" (emphasis added).

God doesn't only want us to produce fruit—he wants fruit that abides and makes a long-term difference in the lives of others. What does abiding fruit look like? The Greek word for *abide* in verse 16 is the same as we saw throughout the text: μένω (*menō*), which can also be translated as to "remain," "endure," and "continue." Our fruit, or the results of all our work, should have longevity. It is intended to ripen into eternity.

That might be easier to picture if you teach a Bible class, do missionary work, or are involved in a nonprofit. But what about folding the laundry? Bringing in the mail to an elderly neighbor? Cleaning? Paying bills? Answering phone calls? Running a business? What do these types of work have to do with eternity? Colossians 3:17 says, "Whatever you do, in word or deed, do everything in the name of the Lord Jesus, giving thanks to God the Father through him." All our work matters to God, and all our work benefits from rest, as we see in God's pattern of work and rest.

Think through your week. What tasks feel mundane? What tasks feel like they're too much? Go to God and tell him how you feel about your work. Ask him to reveal if anything on your plate is excess or unnecessary. Then ask him to give you an eternal perspective in the work he has called you to.

## The Roots

Let us not grow weary of doing good, for in due season we will reap, if we do not give up. (Galatians 6:9)

Weary | ἐκκακέω | *ekkakeō* | ek-kak-eh'-o | faint, utterly spiritless, exhausted

Good | καλός | *kalos* | kal-os' | honorable, honest, excellent

Reap | θερίζω | *therizō* | ther-id'-zo | harvest

## Rest & Reflect

As children of God, our work should reflect our Creator and be honorable, honest, and excellent. If we read this verse with a hustle mindset, we might think we must press on and persevere in *our* strength. Whenever you hear or read this verse, remember God's provisions for weariness. How do we "not grow weary" in our work? By abiding in God's presence and faithfully pressing on in his power as we trust him for the results. Like fruit pausing on the grapevine, ask God to help you abide and rest in his presence as he prepares you for future growth and to produce fruit that lasts.

## Under the Microscope

In week 4 we looked at the first two verses of Psalm 92, which is titled "A Song for the Sabbath." Let's look at the psalm again, but this time at verses 12–15, where fruit is mentioned. This inclusion of fruit, or the result of our works, in a psalm for Sabbath beautifully points to how rest upholds our work. Sabbath and rest are essential to fruit that abides. Read the passage and follow the steps below:

- Circle the word *flourish* in verses 12 and 13. Next to *flourish* write "sprout, bud, bloom, blossom, grow."
- Underline *house of the* LORD and *courts of our God* in verse 13. Next to the underlined words write "Christ dwells inside of me."

### PSALM 92:12–15

[12] The righteous flourish like the palm tree
    and grow like a cedar in Lebanon.
[13] They are planted in the house of the LORD;
    they flourish in the courts of our God.
[14] They still bear fruit in old age;
    they are ever full of sap and green,
[15] to declare that the LORD is upright;
    he is my rock, and there is no unrighteousness in him.

- In what area are you frustrated with a lack of results?
- How might going to God with your concerns and resting in his presence help?
- Write a prayer asking God to grow your faith in specific ways or to bear fruit in a specific work or endeavor. Boldly

ask him to give you a glimpse of the results he is working out. Ask him to help you abide and remain in his presence as he brings forth lasting fruit in and through you.

# WEEK 6

## Day 5

# WHAT DOES A LIFE
# AT REST LOOK LIKE?

I HOPE THAT MOVING FORWARD, you'll look at nature and see restful rhythms. If you happen upon a hummingbird zipping from one blossom to the next or hovering over a feeder, reflect on their torpor strategy of deep, regular rest. And when you see a caterpillar waiting in its chrysalis, may it remind you of the necessity of restful waiting. The next time you see a bird flying across the sky, recall how the great frigate bird rests midair, remaining in flight for up to two months, filtering out unnecessary information so it can focus on what's vital. I hope tree roots winding along a path remind you of the roots of rest that spread throughout Scripture and creation.

Nature thrives through rest, and we are created to do likewise. But what does a life at rest look like? How can you know when you have succeeded in this countercultural journey of biblical rest? We will never fully arrive at perfect rest and peace until we enter God's full presence in eternity. However, we have already seen how biblical rest and spiritual growth work together.

We are not simply addressing chronic fatigue or overwhelm. This is not an energy hack. Instead, we are taking essential and powerful steps toward becoming who God made us to be. As we wrap up our study, I want to give you a key indicator question for when you wonder, *Am I living at rest?* Ask yourself, *Am I growing in truth and love?* Do you remember the perennial plants we studied during week 1? While at rest, their roots strengthen, and the plant grows back bigger and more brilliant each year. Rest should have the same effect in our lives. Growing in truth and love are evidence of a life at rest.

This week we've studied the theme of *abiding* in John 15. This passage also speaks about the vital work of growing in truth and love. Why do you think this passage relates the concepts of abiding, truth, and love? As we rest and abide in Christ, truth and love will flourish.

The roots of truth and love run deep and wide in Scripture and intertwine with the roots of rest. Let's consider first how rest and truth are connected. John 15:3 declares we are made clean by God's Word. We can see this also in John 17:17: "Sanctify them in the truth; your word is truth." God's truth has a cleansing and sanctifying effect, and we experience it as we practice resting in his presence. As we rest, we grow in truth. John 15:7 talks about God's Word abiding in us, and Colossians 3:16 says, "Let the word of Christ dwell in you richly." As we rest in him, his word rests or dwells in us and flourishes, affecting our attitudes, habits, and behaviors. How has Christ's Word of Truth made you clean? How is he currently transforming and growing you through his Word of Truth?

Rest grows us in love as well as truth. John 15:9 encourages us to abide in Christ's love. His love for us is unconditional and unchanging, but we can experience it to varying levels, depending on how well we rest in his presence. The outpouring of Christ's love in us results in love for others. John 15:12 says, "This is my commandment, that you love one another as I have loved you." As we rest in Christ's love, we're better able to love others.

So are you growing in truth and love? This maturation of faith doesn't come through our own efforts and forcefulness but instead through rest. As we spend time in *erēmos*, celebrate Sabbath, form our days around selah pauses, and abide in God's restful presence, growing in truth and love is the natural outcome, all by God's design.

## The Roots

> We were buried therefore with him by baptism into death, in order that, just as Christ was raised from the dead by the glory of the Father, we too might walk in newness of life. (Romans 6:4)

Raised | ἐγείρω | *egeirō* | eg-i'-ro | to lift up (often used to describe resurrection and new life)

Walk | περιπατέω | *peripateō* | per-ee-pat-eh'-o | make one's way, regulate life, conduct oneself

Newness | καινότης | *kainotēs* | kahee-not'-ace | a new state of being

## Rest & Reflect

How might God want to bring you into a new state of being through restful rhythms and practices?

This passage speaks to our eternal salvation through Christ but also alludes to a new experience and way to regulate life and conduct oneself. What old ways of exhaustion, hurry, and pining for control might Jesus be calling us to bury and leave behind? What vital role might rest play as we live in the newness of life that Christ made possible? How might this new way of life grow us in truth and love? Reflect on the past six weeks of studying God's design and heart for rest. How has he already helped you to put away former things, such as habits of hurry or restless living? What new routines and life-giving rhythms is he calling you to or has he already brought you into? Take time to stop and reflect on the growth you've already experienced and to delight in the newness of life God is inviting you into.

### Under the Microscope

God is the bringer of new life and a refresher of hope. As we return to God's pattern of rest and grow in truth and love, read Isaiah 43:18–19 and follow the steps below:

- Underline *former things* and *things of old*. Beside these, write old ways, habits, or tendencies you want to ask God to remove, such as "rush," "hurry," "anxiety," or "need for control."
- Circle *new thing* and next to it write words that capture your desire for a more restful life, perhaps "peace," "unhurried," "abiding," "calm," "quiet," "focused," "fruitful." You might also write a prayer asking God to produce these things in you through rest.
- Underline *rivers in the desert* and write next to it "Psalm 23:2, restful waters" and "John 4:13–14, living water."

## ISAIAH 43:18–19

[18] Remember not the former things,
    nor consider the things of old.
[19] Behold, I am doing a new thing;
    now it springs forth, do you not perceive it?
I will make a way in the wilderness
    and rivers in the desert.

These words were spoken to the Israelites. However, in this text we glimpse God's heart for all his children, including us. God helps us put away what is old and unhelpful, such as hurry, stress, and anxiety, and offers us a new, thriving reality supported by rest. As you practice rest (as messy and imperfect as it will be at times), remember that God is doing a new thing. He will make a way in the wilderness and rivers in the desert. Something new is springing forth.

# WEEK 6

*Days 6 and 7*

# STOP & DELIGHT

## CHECK IN ON TRUTH AND LOVE

ABIDE WITH JESUS. GO WITH him to your *erēmos* place or sit with him on Sabbath, and bring a notebook. Take a deep, helpful look at your current reality. Can you see truth growing, or are you struggling to hear God's voice above the Enemy's lies or society's noise? Can you see love flourishing, or is a preoccupation with productivity and neglect of rest turning your thoughts toward self rather than others? Don't be discouraged if you can't see evidence of growth. Remember that his restful presence is the remedy, and sometimes the roots have to grow before we see any sprouts above ground.

As you stop and spend time abiding with Jesus, delight in his endless reservoir of truth and love. Thank him for his written truth, the Bible, the myriad ways he reveals himself in nature, and for how he makes himself known in us through the Spirit. Delight in his love that, without fail, always invites us into his restful presence.

Ask him to continuously pour truth and love into you.

Ready to exhale?

It is time to rest.

## Journaling Questions

In what ways might God be calling you to practice staying? Do you need to stay and rest in his presence through grief? Do you need to pause and regroup before committing to a responsibility or starting something new? Is he nudging you to dial back your pace so you can linger with loved ones?

What do you need God's restful presence to go with you into? Are you facing a decision or entering into something new? Ask God to accompany you and keep you at rest through whatever challenges and changes may come.

What fruit, or results, is your life yielding? Ask God to produce in you the lasting fruit of truth and love as you practice abiding in his restful presence.

# ACKNOWLEDGMENTS

Thank you to our Creator God, who masterfully designed every wonderful thing in creation and causes it all to thrive through rest. Thank you for graciously taking me out of half-dead living and proving to me that rest is realistic, relevant, and available. Thank you for every Sabbath spent in the sun with a good book, lots of coffee, and my favorite people.

Thank you to Grayson for convincing me to rest and calling me back to rest whenever work tempts me away from it. Thank you for sleeping in on Saturdays, for family brunches, and for gathering and keeping our family together around this shared experience of Sabbath.

Thank you, Zeke, Ellis, Will, and Roary, for diving into Sabbath with excitement. Thank you for your enthusiasm to spend time together as a family and for every walk together to find monarch caterpillars and Lazuli buntings.

Thank you to my technical editors who offered invaluable insight into the science, nature, and theology of this work. Thank you, Jason Weaver, for your patience years ago when I failed your Greek class in Bible college—and your help all these years later with the Greek and Hebrew in this book.

Thank you, David Williams, for your insight into Hebrews 3–4 and your time and care in reading this manuscript.

Thank you, Michael Lane, for your careful reading and fascinating insight and your additions to the nature analogies throughout this work. Thank you for taking Grayson on a marine biology trip years ago (which he still often talks about) and for all the ways you are pointing the next generation to the evidence for God in creation with Evidence 4 Faith.

Thank you, Jill Smith, for your shared enthusiasm about God's creation and teaching others through it. I'm so glad God nudged me to pick up your incredible book *Nature Unveiled* in the bookstore. Your time and attention to the details of this work were above and beyond what I could have asked for.

Thank you to Jenny, Becca, and Bri for prayerfully reading through the early stages of this manuscript and lending your honest feedback. Your friendship is dear, and I love walking through this restful life with you.

Thank you to my mom, Arlene, whose trips to Colorado are becoming all the more frequent. You make my work possible. Thank you for embracing the role of Hammy Poppins and loving on the kids so well, which allows me the gift of rest during my most busy seasons. Thank you for carefully reading all my manuscripts.

Thank you to my dad, Alan, for lending us Mom when I need her. Thank you for showing me the details of creation and all the many ways they prove there is a Creator. You have strengthened my faith through science.

Thank you, Scott and Chris, for raising a man who cares about the things God cares about and who isn't afraid to live counterculturally and raise his family to do likewise. Thank you for instilling in him a love for the lake life.

Thank you to Bob Hostetler of The Steve Laube Agency, Janyre Tromp, Dori Harrell, and the Kregel Publications team for seeing the need for this work and making it a reality.

# NOTES

### What Is Vital?

1. *The Complete Works of Oswald Chambers* (Discovery House, 2000), 946, emphasis added.

### Week 1—Day 1

1. Watchman Nee, *Sit, Walk, Stand* (Tyndale House, 1977), 16.
2. *Thayer's Greek Lexicon*, "G4520—sabbatismos," Blue Letter Bible, accessed January 3, 2025, https://www.blueletterbible.org/lexicon/g4520/kjv/tr/0-1/.

### Week 1—Day 2

1. Joan E. Strassmann, *Slow Birding: The Art and Science of Enjoying the Birds in Your Own Backyard* (TarcherPerigee, 2022), 157.
2. Gregg Davidson and Kenneth J. Turner, *The Manifold Beauty of Genesis One: A Multi-Layered Approach* (Kregel Academic, 2021), 147.
3. Dave Williams, guest, *Strong by Design*, podcast, episode 272, "How to Find REST," Team CriticalBench, February 15, 2023, https://www.strongbydesignpodcast.com/podcast/ep-272-how-to-find-rest-ft-dave-williams/.

### Week 1—Day 3

1. John Mark Comer, *The Ruthless Elimination of Hurry: How to Stay Emotionally Healthy and Spiritually Alive in the Chaos of the Modern World* (WaterBrook, 2019), 155.

# Notes

## Week 1—Day 5

1. John Muir, *My First Summer in the Sierra* (Houghton Mifflin, 1911), 211.
2. Cassandra D. Gould van Praag et al., "Mind-Wandering and Alterations to Default Mode Network Connectivity when Listening to Naturalistic Versus Artificial Sounds," *Scientific Reports* 7, no. 45273 (2017), https://doi.org/10.1038/srep45273.
3. Maltbie Davenport Babcock, "This Is My Father's World," originally written as a poem and published (posthumously) in 1901, set to music by Franklin L. Sheppard in 1915, public domain.

## Week 2—Day 2

1. Robert Robinson, "Come Thou Fount of Every Blessing," public domain.

## Week 2—Day 4

1. Paul Barnett, *The Message of 2 Corinthians: Power in Weakness*, The Bible Speaks Today (InterVarsity Press, 1988), 113.

## Week 2—Day 5

1. Peter Wohlleben, *The Hidden Life of Trees: What They Feel, How They Communicate; Discoveries from a Secret World*, trans. Jane Billinghurst (David Suzuki Institute; Greystone Books, 2016), 142.

## Week 3—Day 1

1. Saint Augustine of Hippo, *The Confessions of Saint Augustine* (Doubleday, 1960), 43.

## Week 4—Day 2

1. James B. Maas, *Power Sleep: The Revolutionary Program That Prepares Your Mind for Peak Performance* (Villard, 1998), 7.
2. Bruce Barton, *The Man Nobody Knows: A Discovery of the Real Jesus* (Bobbs-Merrill, 1925), 77, italics in the original.

3. Nor Amira Syahira Mohd Azmi et al., "Cortisol on Circadian Rhythm and Its Effect on Cardiovascular System," *International Journal of Environmental Research and Public Health* 18, no. 2 (2021), https://doi.org/10.3390/ijerph18020676.

## Week 4—Day 3

1. Jo-Ann Shelton, *As the Romans Did: A Sourcebook in Roman Social History*, 2nd ed. (Oxford University Press, 1998), 124.

## Week 5—Day 3

1. Matthew Sleeth, *24/6: A Prescription for a Healthier, Happier Life* (Tyndale House, 2012), 119.

## Week 5—Day 5

1. Matthew Sleeth, *24/6: A Prescription for a Healthier, Happier Life* (Tyndale House, 2012), 102.

## Week 6—Day 1

2. John Piper, "If You Abide in My Word, You Are Truly My Disciples," Desiring God, April 16, 2011, https://www.desiringgod.org/messages/if-you-abide-in-my-word-you-are-truly-my-disciples, italics in the original.

# ABOUT THE AUTHOR

 Eryn Lynum is a certified master naturalist, educator, national speaker, and author of *Rooted in Wonder: Nurturing Your Family's Faith Through God's Creation* and *936 Pennies: Discovering the Joy of Intentional Parenting.* She hosts the popular podcast for kids, *Nat Theo: Nature Lessons Rooted in the Bible.* She lives in northern Colorado with her husband, Grayson, and their four children, whom they homeschool. She has been featured on broadcasts including Focus on the Family, FamilyLife Today, Christian Parenting, and Raising Christian Kids. Every opportunity she gets, she is out exploring God's creation with her family and sharing the adventures at erynlynum.com.

# Also available from Eryn Lynum

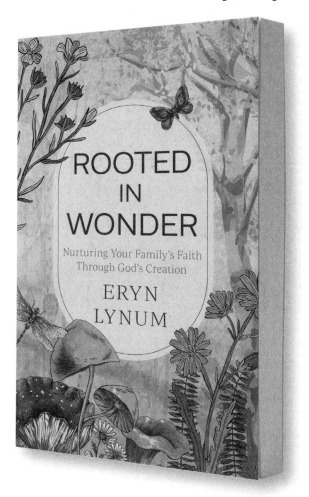

In a screen-focused world, encountering nature—and understanding how God is present in it—is increasingly challenging. Eryn Lynum, a certified master naturalist, Bible teacher, and mother of four, aims to help families rediscover the connection between God and creation. In *Rooted in Wonder*, she shares her journey of getting her kids outdoors and invites parents to do the same. With practical insights on exploring nature through the Bible, including activities related to plants, animals, water, and sky, this guide helps children develop a lasting sense of wonder and faith in their Creator.

**Available wherever books
and ebooks are sold.**

# YOU CAN KEEP THIS BOOK MOVING!

**Give** this book as a gift.

**Recommend** this book to a friend or group.

**Leave a review** on Christianbook, Goodreads, Amazon, or your favorite bookseller's website.

**Connect** with the author on their social media/website.

**Share** the QR code link on your social media.

2450 Oak Industrial Dr NE | Grand Rapids, MI 49505 | kregel.com

  Follow @kregelbooks

*Our mission as a Christian publisher is to develop and distribute—with integrity and excellence—trusted, biblically based resources that lead individuals to know and serve Jesus Christ.*